FINDING OURSELVES LOST

Finding Ourselves
L O S T

Ministry in the
Age of Overwhelm

Robert C. Dykstra

 CASCADE *Books* • Eugene, Oregon

FINDING OURSELVES LOST
Ministry in the Age of Overwhelm

Pickwick Publications
An Imprint of Wipf and Stock Publishers
199 W. 8th Ave., Suite 3
Eugene, OR 97401

www.wipfandstock.com

PAPERBACK ISBN: 978-1-5326-3481-9
HARDCOVER ISBN: 978-1-5326-3483-3
EBOOK ISBN: 978-1-5326-3482-6

Cataloging-in-Publication data:

Names: Dykstra, Robert C., 1956–, author.

Title: Finding ourselves lost : ministry in the age of overwhelm / Robert C. Dykstra.

Description: Eugene, OR: Cascade Books, 2018. | Includes bibliographical references and index.

Identifiers: ISBN: 978-1-5326-3481-9 (paperback). | ISBN: 978-1-5326-3483-3 (hardcover). | ISBN: 978-1-5326-3482-6 (ebook).

Subjects: LCSH: Pastoral theology.

Classification: BV4011 D95 2018 (print). | BV4011 (ebook).

Manufactured in the U.S.A.   JUNE 11, 2018

The author wishes to express appreciation to Springer Publications for permission to use material from his works previously published in *Pastoral Psychology*: "Finding Ourselves Lost," 59 (2010) 737–46; "Unrepressing the Kingdom: Pastoral Theology as Aesthetic Imagination," 61 (2012) 391–410; "Zombie Alleluias: Learning to Live in the Space Between Worlds," 63 (2014) 611–24; "Finding Language for What Matters Most: Hosting Conversations about Sexuality in Pastoral Counseling," 64 (2015) 663–80; "Meet the Terrible Resistance: Childhood Suffering and the Christian Body," 65 (2016) 657–68; and "The Sacredness of Individuality: Introspection for Refuting States of Total Conviction in Boys and Men," 66 (2017) 779–97. The author also wishes to thank Walter de Gruyter for permission to use Robert C. Dykstra, "Wedding of the Waters: Pastoral Theological Reflections on the Self," previously published in the *International Journal of Practical Theology* 2 (1999) 251–68; the National Portrait Gallery of the Smithsonian Institution, Washington, DC, for permission to use the portrait of William James by artist John La Farge, c. 1860, oil on cardboard, gift of William James IV;

For Eleanor and Annie

"Saruman believes it is only great power that can hold evil in check. But that is not what I have found. I have found it is the small things, everyday deeds of ordinary folk, that keeps the darkness at bay. Simple acts of kindness and love."

—GANDALF TO GALADRIEL,
THE HOBBIT: AN UNEXPECTED JOURNEY (JACKSON, 2012)

Contents

Acknowledgments

I wish to thank K. C. Hanson, editor-in-chief of Cascade Books, and the entire Cascade team—especially Matthew Wimer, assistant managing editor; Brian Palmer, editorial assistant; Jeremy Funk, copy editor; Heather Carraher, typesetter; James Stock, marketing director; and Shannon Carter, who designed the cover—for their diligence and generosity of spirit at each stage of the publication process.

I initially offered the essays of this book either as lectures with my students and for alumni/ae gatherings of Princeton Theological Seminary or as conference papers with professional colleagues in the Group for New Directions in Pastoral Theology, the Association for Clinical Pastoral Education, and the Philadelphia Group for Pastoral Theology with Boys and Men. The thoughtful responses of those students and friends over many years have served as no less than redemptive lifelines for me. I am grateful as well to former students for permission to share portions of their life stories in these pages.

Because, as is evident in these pages, my own work and thought have long drawn inspiration from the work and thought of my colleague and friend Donald Capps, who died suddenly in August of 2015 in the aftermath of a car accident in Princeton, I want to thank in particular Karen Capps, John Capps, and Nathan Carlin for helping to sustain me through our mutual season of grief. Molly Dykstra, beloved companion and steady friend, continues daily to imbue in me courage to face the mysteries.

I dedicate this book to our daughters Eleanor and Annie, beacons of light who in small things and everyday deeds help keep the darkness at bay.

Introduction

The essays of this book explore the significance of pastoral theology for ministries of care and counseling in what psychotherapist Mary Pipher (2015) calls "the age of overwhelm."

Pipher describes a kind of "primal panic" in her clients arising from "daily bombardment of information overload" and a sense of helplessness amid vast global threats of climate change or terrorism. Human beings simply are not built, she says, "to absorb, process, and act on the amount of information we get every day. The result is that we're warier and more compartmentalized than ever before" (p. 22).

She cites the research of British anthropologist Alex Bentley and colleagues (Spiegel, 2013), who used computers to search out the frequency of words expressing various emotional states found in a wide range of printed literature from the early twentieth century to the present. The investigators were surprised to discover that all such emotional "words about sadness and joy and anger and disgust and surprise" appeared less frequently in our era than a century earlier, with just one exception: *fear*. "The fear-related words start to increase just before the 1980s," Bentley notes, a trend that continued until 2008, the final year of the study.

Recent data from Amazon may reinforce Pipher's and Bentley's observations regarding the age of overwhelm. In 2014, the company reported that the most widely highlighted Bible passage in its Kindle e-readers was Philippians 4:6–7 (NIV): "Do not be anxious about anything, but in every situation, by prayer and petition, with thanksgiving, present your requests to God. And the peace of God, which transcends all understanding, will guard your hearts and your minds in Christ Jesus" (Meyer, 2014). But I wonder, might not relief from anxiety sought by Kindle users in these Scripture verses be offset by anxiety that arises from knowing Amazon tracks those passages they highlight?

The chapters that follow represent my own various efforts—as a person, as a Christian minister, as a pastoral theologian—to wrestle with and respond to the quandaries of finding ourselves lost in an age of overwhelm. Most chapters stem from lectures presented to audiences of seminary students and ministers or, in some cases, of academic theologians and professional pastoral counselors. They were written for the ear as much as for the eye. Although each chapter stands on its own as a discrete work, a number of core principles or convictions, four of which I introduce here, recur throughout the book as vital to my own understanding of pastoral theology and its impact on ministries of care.

In a previous book, *Images of Pastoral Care* (Dykstra, 2005), I discussed how elusive any firm definition of pastoral theology or precise description of the tasks of ministry has proven to be. This tenuousness reflects the impossible vocation of theologians and ministers, compelled to speak of an unspeakable God and to seek meaning and hope amid inexplicable loss. "Both the madness and wisdom of pastoral theology and its resulting approaches to pastoral care and counseling," I wrote there, "derive from keen attention to life on the boundaries, making pastoral theology's . . . frequent identity confusion less its burden than its calling and destiny" (p. 4). As a result, pastoral theologians and ministers alike tend to employ "indirection, analogy, even poetry" to describe what they do; "anything short of this would mock the complexity of the human heart and mind and disregard the limitations of any individual perspective on the perplexities of the human condition" (p. 5).

Despite these genuine ambiguities, students in seminary classrooms, not unlike parishioners in pews or hospital beds, expect and deserve from their teacher or minister at least *some* word, however halting, to guide their interests or salve their wounds. To this end, in the chapters that follow I attempt to convey, through various means of indirection, my sense of the nature and purpose of pastoral theology. My zeal for this remarkable discipline has been unflagging over decades of teaching. My hope is that in these pages its appeal might also prove contagious and edifying to readers.

Speaking What Cannot Be Spoken

One long-standing conviction in particular recurs again and again as a refrain in this pursuit—namely, that *to the extent seminarians and ministers find the courage and resources necessary to explore their own debilitating childhood shame, they gain empathy and skill for assisting others in their pastoral care.* This is because, as pastoral theologian Donald Capps (1983) once wrote, "as we cross the boundary from avoiding shame to embracing it, accepting it as the most intimate part of ourselves, we create the inner climate in which God becomes revealed to us" (p. 91). Capps, whose work figures prominently throughout this book, bases his claim on Jesus' death as a common criminal in full public view, a shame "of the most excruciating kind": "To put our shameful selves aside is to dissociate ourselves experientially from the shame of the cross. To embrace our shameful self is to identify with Jesus and thereby experience God as no longer hidden" (p. 92).

A recent exemplar for me of Capps's directive to embrace one's shame has been Domingo Martinez (2012), whose first book, *The Boy Kings of Texas*, was a finalist for the National Book Award in 2012. Until the time of his award nomination at age forty, Martinez was selling business cards at an obscure print shop in a small town north of Seattle. His book is a raw and unsparing memoir of a hardscrabble childhood of poverty, racism, and alcohol-fueled abuse on the South Texas border. Asked by a reporter (Tillman, 2012) how he managed to write of his childhood with such naked transparency, Martinez responded: "I was drawn toward the pain . . . If the memory felt uncomfortable, if it was something I knew our family didn't talk about, I'd attack it head-on." Chapter by brutally honest chapter, attack he does. He told the reporter that "the reservoir of anger that propelled [him] through the writing process had dissipated by the time he finished the book." During that time, he also saw a therapist.

The strategy that restored Martinez to himself and in turn enthralled his readers—focusing on the pain, speaking what in childhood could not be spoken—corroborates Capps's claim that as we embrace shame as the most intimate part of ourselves, God may be revealed to us, healing may come. In the lectures that make up this book, I invite listeners, often implicitly, at times explicitly, to read—but also to write, to speak—their own stories of suffering into the story of God. Engaging in this kind of unrepentant eisegesis enables us to "experience God as no longer hidden" and thereby to loathe ourselves less, to feel less alone in the world. Helping ourselves and others to desist for a moment from self-loathing and to feel less lonely strikes me as central to the work of pastoral theology and ministry.

More or Less Lonely?

In his memoir *Just Like Someone Without Mental Illness Only More So*, Mark Vonnegut (2010), a celebrated Boston pediatrician and son of novelist Kurt Vonnegut, describes his personal struggles with bipolar disorder. These included several psychotic episodes that required hospitalization at various intervals in his early adult life and beyond. After publishing a book in his midtwenties recounting his experiences with psychosis to that point (Vonnegut 2002), he decided at age twenty-eight that he wanted to go to medical school. Despite his undergraduate GPA of 1.8 in math and the sciences and having been rejected by nineteen other medical schools, he was admitted, against all odds and just four years after his hospitalization, to Harvard Medical School (Vonnegut, 2010, p. 62). In his more recent memoir, written from the vantage of his sixties, Vonnegut reflects on the improbability, even in the 1970s, of his admission to any medical school, let alone Harvard, but also on how his admission would be inconceivable in today's frenzied academic climate. Had he not been admitted to Harvard Medical School, Boston would have been deprived over the past decades of a wise and acclaimed pediatrician and clinical professor of medicine.

At some point Vonnegut was enlisted to conduct admissions interviews for applicants to Harvard Medical School. He came to lament in this role how indistinguishable they all seemed. "They were all bright and earnest and planning to help people," he said. "I hurried them through all that because I couldn't tell one from the other. 'Yes, yes, yes . . . but what exactly is being a doctor going to do for you?'" he wanted them to tell (p. 78). His eventual criterion for discerning between them? "What I asked myself about applicants," he says, "was whether talking to them made me more or less lonely" (p. 66).

Recently I was eating lunch with another professor in the seminary dining room. A student soon joined us and a lively exchange ensued. But then a seminary administrator sat down at our table and proceeded to commandeer the conversation. After the lunch I recalled Vonnegut's gut admissions-interview benchmark, and I came to realize that in this colleague's presence I tended to feel more rather than less lonely. It was somehow satisfying to be able to use Vonnegut's test to name this feeling.

Vonnegut's little gut check for medical school applicants leads to a second recurring conviction, augmenting the first, in the present book—namely, that when seminary students, ministers, or parishioners manage to summon the courage to revisit their childhood suffering and shame and then dare to reveal what they find to a trusted confidant, *they should feel less lonely rather than lonelier for having done so.* To my way of thinking, pastoral theology and ministries of pastoral care and counseling involve helping people feel better. Vonnegut's experience interviewing prospective medical students suggests that to the extent our work helps others or ourselves to feel better, to feel less lonely, it is on a productive path.

Attending to Differences That Fuel Isolation

Therapeuo is a biblical word, Greek for "I cure" or "I heal" or "I serve" (see Luke 12:42; Acts 17:25), and it occurs dozens of times in the New Testament. Jesus' own inordinate attention to healing and serving was a distinguishing mark of his ministry. *Therapeuo*—from which, of course, we derive the word "therapy"—is no dubious practice for Jesus. It is, rather, precisely what he does, his line of work. It defines his life and ministry.

But this therapeutic work is not exclusive to Jesus. He instructs his followers, too, to pursue it. An overlooked narrative bridge consisting of just two verses in the Gospel of Luke (9:10–11) links far more familiar and extensive accounts of Jesus sending his disciples on the mission of the twelve (9:1–6), on the one hand, and his feeding of the five thousand (9:12–17), on the other. The brief transitional passage between these two texts recounts Jesus' invitation to his disciples, newly christened as *apostles* ("sent ones") after their successful mission trip, for a time away with him. Their retreat, however, is short-lived, for "when the crowds found out about it, they followed [Jesus]; and he welcomed them, and spoke to them about the kingdom of God, and healed those who needed to be cured" (9:11). The elegant simplicity of the three verbs describing Jesus' actions in response to the crowds—*welcomed, spoke,* and *healed* (reflecting pastoral tasks of compassion, teaching, and therapy)—captures the central thrust of his ministry (see also Luke 4:18, 40–44; 6:17–18; 8:1–2). But these are the very same tasks he previously had assigned to his disciples as they were about to depart on the mission of the twelve.

In addition to instructions about hospitality, Jesus "gave them power and authority over all demons and to cure diseases, and he sent them out to proclaim the kingdom of God and to heal" (Luke 9:1–2): the disciples, too, were directed to welcome, speak, and heal. As New Testament scholar Joel B. Green (1997) notes regarding the transitional narrative of Luke 9:11: "This summary of [Jesus'] ministry is indistinguishable from the ministry in which the twelve had participated (vv. 1–2, 6)—a reality that serves at least initially to blur even further any possible lines of distinction between their activity on God's behalf and [Jesus'] own" (p. 362). Jesus is portrayed here as assuming that the work of *therapeuo*—of healing, curing, serving— is something that, like tasks of hospitality and proclamation, can be taught to and learned by those who minister in his name. According to Green, "The twelve are described as persons involved in the two primary foci of Jesus' missionary activity—proclaiming the good news of the kingdom and healing those who are sick and demonized" (pp. 358–59).

Despite Jesus' assumption of correspondence between his work and theirs, however, there has developed over recent decades a kneejerk reaction against contemporary pastoral theology, along with the therapeutic strategies it engenders, especially among learned theologians and the spiritual elite, for whom "therapy" has become a tainted word, a spiritually suspect practice. Theological detractors of *therapeuo* furrow their brows at any enterprise that hints of drawing on psychology in particular or of attending to the needs of individuals over the concerns of wider communities—emphases long associated with contemporary pastoral theology. Their disdain may simply reflect an extension to certain theologians of H. L. Mencken's (1949/1982, p. 624) classic definition of Puritanism, as "the haunting fear that someone, somewhere, may be happy." Whatever its source, this cloud hovers over the discipline of pastoral theology even as it casts its shadow on the day-to-day work of pastoral care and counseling. Even Vonnegut's sense of having felt less lonely for talking with someone would be likely to raise eyebrows among religious professionals. Spiritual direction? By all means, yes, they would say. "Christian" or so-called "biblical" counseling? Of course. Dynamic pastoral theology or psychotherapy? Not so much.

I recall the impact on me two decades ago of reading two simple questions posed by Capps (1993, pp. 114–15) in response to what sociologist Robert Bellah and others (1985) were decrying at that time as a rampant "expressive individualism" and the so-called "triumph of the therapeutic" (Rieff, 1966/2006) in American cultural life. In a chapter titled "Expressive Individualism as Scapegoat" in *The Depleted Self*, Capps (1993) methodically counters these critiques of individualism, notably by challenging the way Bellah and others read Ralph Waldo Emerson (1946/1981, pp. 72–91, 138–64) in, for example, "Self-Reliance" and the "Divinity School Address" on the purposes and possibilities of the individual in American life. "Emerson would not have devoted so much attention to the problem of social conformity, especially its destructive effects on one's inner character," Capps (1993, p. 109) writes, "if he did not assume that the individual would also be an active participant in social life."

But even more so than by Bellah and colleagues, Capps finds himself vexed by theologians who reflexively rush to baptize Bellah's criticisms of the therapeutic. As one example, C. Ellis Nelson (1989), in his book *How Faith Matures*, draws on Bellah to denounce the modern sense that "authority is [no longer] in God, who comes into a person's life with a mission; it is rooted in a person's psychological needs . . . The search is not for truth about God but for religious beliefs and practices that help people cope with inner difficulties or provide a way to make sense of the variety of events taking place around them" (p. 38).

Capps (1993) in turn proceeds to raise the two questions to Nelson that have long influenced my own vocational quest: "What is so wrong," Capps wants to know, "with churches helping people cope with inner difficulties and make sense of events taking place around them? And why assume that divine authority and human mission is incommensurate with our psychological needs?" (p. 115).

This disaffection for pastoral care and counseling among prominent Christian theologians continues unabated. A more recent instance is found in criticism offered by William H. Willimon (2013), professor of the practice of ministry at Duke Divinity School, concerning the priorities of ministers formerly under his supervision as a United Methodist bishop:

> My admiration is unbounded for clergy who persist in proclaiming the gospel in the face of the resistance that the world throws at them. But I found too many clergy who allowed congregational caregiving and maintenance to trump more important acts of ministry, like truth telling and mission leadership. These tired pastors dash about offering parishioners undisciplined compassion rather than sharp biblical truth. One pastor led a self-study of her congregation and found that 80 percent of them thought that the minister's primary job was to 'care for me and my family.' Debilitation is predictable for a *kleros* with no higher purpose for ministry than servitude to the voracious personal needs of the *laos*. (p. 11)

Capps's response to Nelson's charges applies equally to Willimon's: Why assume that congregational caregiving and maintenance, or pastoral compassion and attention to the personal needs of parishioners, are incommensurate with biblical truth and mission leadership?

Capps's questions have led me again and again over the years to shout into the wind that *therapeuo*—healing, curing, serving—is divinely blessed: it is not just an essential aspect of Jesus' ministry but his aspiration for our own. We should honor, not disdain, those moments when individuals—when we ourselves as seminarians and ministers, as when those to whom we offer care and counsel—come to feel, with Vonnegut, less lonely rather than lonelier for having confided in another.

This is not to suggest that therapeutic conversations are without pain and struggle. They involve hard work both for those who provide and those who receive pastoral care and counseling. Sometimes we ourselves as ministers, along with those whom we counsel, may need to feel worse—that is, to begin to feel previously suppressed grief, anxiety, loneliness, or despair—as the path to being able to feel anything at all. In a lengthy profile of Bruce Springsteen in the *New Yorker*, David Remnick (2012) reveals that Springsteen has long used therapy to battle malignant depression but that, in addition, his "creative talent has also been nurtured by the darker currents of his psyche":

> "I'm thirty years in analysis!" [Springsteen] said. "Look, you cannot underestimate the fine power of self-loathing in [my line of work]. You think, I don't like anything I'm seeing. I don't like anything I'm doing, but I need to change myself, I need to transform myself. I do not know a single artist who does not run on that fuel. If you are extremely pleased with yourself, nobody would be f---ing doing it! Brando would not have acted. Dylan wouldn't have written 'Like a Rolling Stone.' James Brown wouldn't have gone 'Unh!' He wouldn't have searched that one-beat down that was so hard. That's a motivation, that element of 'I need to remake myself, my town, my audience'—the desire for renewal." (p. 54)

In therapeutic vulnerability as in artistic creativity, these disconcerting feelings—Springsteen's "fine power of self-loathing," not unlike Martinez's being "drawn toward the pain" or Capps's "embracing our shameful self"—can precipitate a generative capacity for renewal.

But however predictable this trajectory in pastoral conversation and in artistic expression, should not seminarians, ministers, and parishioners alike feel on balance less lonely rather than lonelier for having revealed *even these painful kinds of emotions or memories* to a trusted other, even after just one conversation together? We might therefore ask Vonnegut's question of ourselves as caregivers as a fine means of assessing any given pastoral exchange. It is *okay*, *therapeutic*, even *biblical* to feel better for our having shared this encounter, despite unrelenting efforts of the spiritual elite to suggest otherwise.

Religious professionals critical of those searching for "beliefs and practices that help [them] cope with inner difficulties or provide a way to make sense of the variety of events taking place around them," or who disparage pastors concerned about congregational caregiving, contribute to what Capps (1998, pp. viii, 5–6) describes elsewhere as the current widespread avoidance of pastoral counseling on the part of parish ministers. Rather than seeing pastoral counseling as something "so integral to the ministry of the church that, without it, the Christian life itself is impoverished" (p. 5), parish ministers, if they encourage parishioners to seek counseling at all, choose to "leave it to the professionals, who (apparently) know what they are doing" (p. viii). "While we never even raise the question whether congregational life would be seriously impoverished if there were no preaching," Capps writes, "this 'taken-for-grantedness' does not apply to pastoral counseling" (p. 6). The work of *therapeuo* is seen, if not as unpatriotic or spiritually suspect (as Bellah, Nelson, Willimon, and others convey), then at the very least as optional or beyond the reach or responsibility of ordinary ministers.

But the ministry of Jesus entailed far more than preaching to crowds. He may well have had aspirations for saving humanity as a collective whole, but he rarely appears to have approached his task from the distant perch of what William James (1896/1956, p. 256) disparaged as the "bird's-eye view" of the sociologist, in which vanish the specific details and unique attributes of individuals. Jesus zeroes in on the plights of individuals, such that in his presence the bird's-eye view itself vanishes.

Pastoral theologians have justly accentuated for decades the merits of attending as caregivers to social and contextual realities that shape, delimit, and enhance personal and communal well-being. Their works draw attention to, among other weighty topics, the therapeutic power of connection in community (Doehring, 2015; Dykstra, 2005; Kim, 2009; LaMothe, 2013; McClure, 2010); issues of racial and cultural alienation, justice, and reconciliation (Butler, 2010; Ellison, 2013; Helsel, 2015; Hinds, 2010; Hinds, 2014; Kujawa-Holbrook & Montagno, 2009; Lartey, 2006; Shin, 2012); and sexual and gender differences and concerns (Leslie, 2003; Marshall, 1997; Miller-McLemore & Gill-Austern, 1999; Stevenson-Moessner & Snorton, 2010). One cumulative effect of their research has been to underscore how even the most private of pastoral conversations encompasses, though also threatens to veil, a host of intersecting familial, cultural, and political ties and trajectories. Bonnie J. Miller-McLemore (1996, p. 18) captures the significance of this sweeping contextual sensitivity among pastoral theologians: "Never again will a clinical moment, whether of caring for a woman recovering from hysterectomy or attending to a woman's spiritual life, be understood on intrapsychic grounds alone. These moments are always and necessarily situated within the interlocking, continually evolving threads of which reality is woven and they can be understood in no other way. Psychology alone cannot understand this web."

While I draw without reserve on psychology throughout this book, as does Miller-McLemore (2003, pp. 26–30) in her work, I advocate with her and other colleagues the use of an array of cognate disciplines for pastoral theology and ministries of care. To privilege the historic focus in pastoral theology on the importance of the individual, whether through case studies, biography, or autobiography, is not, as Capps (2014b) has noted, to perceive "the individual in isolation from his or her social, institutional, and cultural contexts and frameworks" (p. 552, n. 2). An eclectic, likely pragmatic, pastoral approach also seems more in keeping with the portrayal of Jesus in the Gospel of Luke. As Green (1997) observes, "The Third Evangelist knows nothing of such dichotomies as those sometimes drawn between social and spiritual or individual and communal" (p. 25).

William James (1896/1956), for his part, likewise acknowledges that both the communal/sociological and the individual/psychological points of view—the sweeping bird's-eye and the intricately detailed—may have their place, in that both are evident in nature. But he more often stakes his claim as a psychologist, as I choose here to stake mine, on pluralism and therefore on attention to detail and difference among those in one's care. He cites "an unlearned carpenter of [his] acquaintance" who "once said in [his] hearing: 'There is very little difference between one man and another; but what little there is, *is very important.*'" James proceeds to acknowledge that "an inch is a small thing" but then refers to the proverb *An inch on a man's nose is much* (pp. 256–57). Recall in this regard Cyrano de Bergerac and the socially isolating difference an inch can make. And readers familiar with the tyrannical Lord Voldemort of the Harry Potter series (see Rowling, 2000, p. 643) will be quick to note that an inch *off* a man's nose is also much. Certain inches actually matter. The differences between us, however minute, signify our unique attributes and abilities as individuals but also often constitute social vulnerabilities that contribute to our shame. Jesus, long antedating William James and fully attuned to the impact of social forces, appears to pay careful attention to them.

The multitudes that often miss the point of his preaching also prove detrimental to his efforts at healing. Sometimes welcoming but at other times ignoring or even shutting out the crowds, Jesus elevates the significance—for him, for his friends, for the kingdom of God—of the distinct specificity of each individual's loneliness and need. If Jesus has interest in transforming entire communities and contexts, his strategy for doing so ordinarily appears to involve *attending to individual differences that fuel social isolation*—a model for ministries of care that constitutes a third core conviction in the present book. Jesus heals in an intimate and exacting way, by focusing on embodied symptoms of shame that derive from social marginalization. He commends his followers to do likewise.

Believing in Those Who Have Faith in Us

In a number of essays that follow, I draw from the Gospel of Luke to consider how the teaching and healing ministries of Jesus may guide our own pastoral work. According to Green (1997), the pervasive focus of this gospel is *salvation*, a theme implicit in the present book's opening and closing chapters on Jesus' parables of the lost and found of Luke 15. But salvation in Luke is of a kind, Green writes, "neither ethereal nor merely future," but instead "embraces life in the present, restoring the integrity of human life, revitalizing human communities, setting the cosmos in order" (p. 24).

While ordering the cosmos may prove to be above the pay grade of most ministers, happily for us in Luke the act of following Jesus entails in large measure more simply *being with* him. To follow is to spend time with him, to befriend him, to emulate him, to become socialized in the ways he socializes with others. Green notes that for Luke this process involves embodying "the inbreaking of the kingdom of God," most visibly through table fellowship and, as noted, through healing ministries with individuals facing shame and isolation at the margins of society (p. 23). Our foray here into Luke's Gospel undergirds a precept I attempt to convey to students in my classroom as also now to readers of this book—that we as ministers, like the one in whose name we serve, have both the capacity and the good fortune to become this kind of healing agent in the lives of those in our pastoral care.

In chapter 5, as one example, we consider Capps's (2008) detailed exploration, in *Jesus the Village Psychiatrist*, of Jesus' particular approach (in Luke 8:40–56) to restoring to life a twelve-year-old girl presumed by all but him to be dead. Her healing, Capps claims, springs from an intense mutual transfer of relational energy and trust between them, leading him to conclude that "we choose life not because we believe in ideas, however compelling these may be, but because we believe in persons, especially those persons who have faith in us. In the meeting of their hands, Jesus had transferred his faith to [the girl] and had given her faith in the future" (p. 124). Jesus heals, in other words, specifically by means of *our capacity to trust his faith in us as individuals.* This leads to a fourth basic conviction of this book—namely, that *healing in ministry comes through embodied expressions of mutual trust.* Restoration derives from believing in others' faith in us, as from others' belief in our faith in them.

Accepting a Lifetime Achievement Award for his long-running children's television program *Mister Rogers' Neighborhood* at the Emmys ceremony in 1997, Fred Rogers (1997), a Presbyterian minister, deflected attention from himself while requesting something of his distinguished audience: "So many people have helped me to come here to this night. Some of you are here, some are far away, and some are even in heaven. All of us have special ones who have loved us into being. Would you just take, along with me, ten seconds to think of the people who have helped you become who you are, those who have cared about you and wanted what was best for you in life? Ten seconds of silence. I'll watch the time." Then for an eternity of silence for live television, Rogers looks at his watch while cameras pan the vast theater to faces of many whose eyes well up with tears. Finally, he says, "Whomever you've been thinking about, how pleased they must be to know the difference you feel they've made."

I have experienced on untold occasions over many years the curative power of another's faith in me, especially at those times I could conjure little faith in myself. I trust that readers too will recall that person—past or present—who believed in, and thereby contributed to revivifying, them. Among these healers I count mentors, friends, students, even authors; some, such as my minister, Henry E. Fawcett, I have known since childhood, while others, like Domingo Martinez or Fred Rogers, I have never met. Prominent among them, evident already, is Donald Capps, my senior colleague in pastoral theology at Princeton Theological Seminary until his sudden death in 2015. Don restored me to myself again and again, usually through shared laughter over lunch in a back booth at Winberies Restaurant in downtown Princeton.

As these and other friends have inculcated their trust in me, so, too, in what are for me the searching and quite personal essays that follow, I hope to convey my genuine confidence in the capacity of ministers to ease the burden of shame and anxiety, and thereby to enhance the flourishing, of others. I know of no higher—or more down-to-earth—calling than this. To embrace our pastoral role as healers is to summon courage to explore our own debilitating shame and dare to speak what in childhood could not be spoken; to reveal our discoveries to a trusted confidant so as to feel less loathsome or lonely; to attend to minute individual differences, in self and other, that fuel social isolation; and to believe in those who believe in us while also inviting others to trust our faith in them. These are paths by which, to channel Mister Rogers, we "love into being" those who find themselves lost in "the age of overwhelm" (Pipher, 2015, pp. 22–23).

1

Finding Ourselves Lost[1]

On her first day at Princeton Theological Seminary, having driven from California to begin her Master of Divinity program, a good friend of mine asked a returning student how to go about getting to New York City from the campus. "Oh, it's easy," he told her. "You take the Dinky by the Wawa."[2]

"The Dinky by the Wawa?" my friend wondered. *On what planet had she landed?* she asked herself that day she landed in Princeton. The Dinky by the Wawa?

What planet, indeed. It was the first time but not the last that she would ask herself that question, the first time but not the last that she would find someone speaking gibberish, the first time but not the last that she would find herself lost at Princeton Seminary.

Even More Confused Than We Seem

All kinds of words, so many strange words, some of them alien for being so familiar—books and shelves and stacks and libraries full of words like "Dinky," which is Greek for "the little engine that could," and "Wawa," which is Hebrew for "help get me through the night"—books and shelves

---

1. A convocation address delivered in Miller Chapel to students and faculty of Princeton Theological Seminary to open the 2009–2010 academic year.

2. The Dinky is the affectionate moniker used by local residents to refer to the tiny two-car New Jersey Transit shuttle train that links the town of Princeton to the main train station at Princeton Junction, three miles away. The Wawa is a twenty-four-hour convenience mart located next to the Dinky station.

and stacks full of words about God, full of *theo-logoi*. Frederick Buechner (1973) once wrote that "theology is the study of God and [God's] ways. For all we know, dung beetles may study [human beings and their] ways and call it humanology. If so, we would probably be more touched and amused than irritated. One hopes that God feels likewise" (p. 91).

But what choice do we have, really, other than to keep on talking about God, to keep on reading and writing about things of which we know so little, what choice but to embark on this impossible vocation? For that is what it is here we do, spilling sweat, ink, and tuition dollars to try to get God right. At a time when their words about God lead some from another faith to fly airplanes into skyscrapers and others from our own to pray publicly for our president's death, it matters what we say about God.

British psychoanalyst Adam Phillips (2005) ends his book *Going Sane: Maps of Happiness*, a book on the nature of sanity, by saying that it would be sane to take "for granted that everyone is even more confused than they seem. Havoc is always wreaked in fast cures for confusion. The sane believe that confusion, acknowledged, is a virtue; and that humiliating another person is the worst thing we ever do. Sanity should not be our word for the alternative to madness; it should refer to whatever resources we have to prevent humiliation" (p. 199). Because "everyone is even more confused than they seem," especially those at Princeton Seminary where we compel ourselves to talk of things we know so little, we may want to take special care here to do all in our power to avoid humiliating others, to avoid confusing them further.

So many words about God. No wonder we find ourselves confused, find ourselves lost here from time to time.

Does God Have Regard for Me?

John McDargh (1995), a psychologist of religion at Boston College, quoting his Benedictine colleague Dom Sebastian Moore, suggests that the "primary and irreducible proposition about human beings . . . is that 'we all desire to be desired by the one we desire.'" Moore writes, "The only serious form of the religious question today is: Is human awareness, when it finds its fulfillment in love, resonating, albeit faintly, with an origin that 'behaves,' infinitely and all-constitutingly, as love behaves?" McDargh continues, "To ask this question in the poetry of the biblical tradition, 'Does God have regard for me?' or 'Am I a source of delight to the Source of my delight?'" (p. 226).

This may be what those many books and shelves and stacks and libraries full of words about God, what you and I who find ourselves lost, are somehow endeavoring to ask: Does God have regard for me? Am I a source of delight to the Source of my delight?

The answer to this question is not always as clear as one might hope at this schoolhouse, for we find ways enough to demean one another here. But if we were to take to heart the words of Jesus' parable of the one lost sheep (Luke 15:1–7)—a parable that would be among the top contenders if I were pressed to choose the gospel within the gospel—the answer, I suspect, would be an unambiguous *yes*. Yes, God has regard for you. Yes, you are a source of delight to the Source of your delight. This parable could go a long way toward helping us acknowledge our confusion, toward keeping us sane, and as a resource to prevent humiliation.

The One or the Many?

There are plenty, especially among my fellow pastoral theologians, who would take me to task for this choice as a gospel within the gospel, despite, or perhaps because of, the fact that the academic discipline of pastoral theology was pioneered by Seward Hiltner and James Lapsley here at Princeton Seminary in large measure on the basis of this very parable. The parable promotes, Hiltner (1958, pp. 19, 68) believed, the "tender and solicitous care" of the shepherd who at times privileges the needs of the one at what increasing numbers of my colleagues fear may be the expense of the larger flock. Almost before Hiltner's ink was dry on the page, Carroll A. Wise (1966) of Garrett Seminary wrote in 1966 that the symbol of the shepherd advocated in Hiltner's "shepherding perspective" is too dated and rural and therefore "cannot have the power for modern [persons that] it had in the first century" (p. 2). It was also, he thought, too patriarchal: "One of the dangers of this [shepherd] symbol," he writes, is that "it can subtly but powerfully convey the idea of the superiority of the pastor over [the] 'sheep'" (p. 2).

In 1981, Scottish ethicist Alastair V. Campbell (1981) charged not that Hiltner's shepherd was too hard or patriarchal, as Wise had argued, but on the contrary too soft and solicitous: "We are forced to conclude," Campbell writes, "that in Hiltner the image [of the shepherd] is little more than a cipher which gives a religious appearance to statements about [pastoral] care derived from quite other sources, notably the faith statements of Rogerian counseling theory" (p. 42). A decade later, pastoral theologian Jeanne Stevenson-Moessner (1991) wrote that "a paradigm other than that of the good shepherd, one with less inherent danger of lone external hierarchical authority, is crucial for the pastoral care of women. [Women] seek a paradigm that avoids the risk of the lone shepherd who can control, cajole, and cavort with the sheep" (p. 201).

Such critiques have only solidified in recent years, not entirely without justification but swelling today to a clarion call among pastoral theologians to forego emphasis on the lone shepherd and one lost sheep in order to attend instead to the larger community and contextual settings of ministry in a pluralistic world (Ramsay, 2004; McClure, 2010). Despite its historical prominence in constituting pastoral theology as a distinctive academic discipline, the parable of the shepherd and the one lost sheep fell on hard times almost from the start and has never fully recovered—a parable too dated, too rural, too hard, too soft, too hierarchical, too clerical, too individualistic, too Rogerian even, too fill-in-the-blank for guiding our understanding and practices of contemporary faith or ministry.

Swimming in a Sea of Faith

We are cautioned on the use of this parable from beyond the ranks of pastoral theology as well. Stanley Hauerwas (2006), in comments on the Gospel of Matthew's version of the parable (Matt 18:12–14), warns that "the parable of the lost sheep is *not about us.*" He appears to contradict himself in the very same sentence, however, by insisting that the parable is instead "about God's unrelenting love of Israel *and those called to be disciples of God's own son*" (p. 164, italics added). But might not we hope to include ourselves among this latter group of disciples, therefore making the parable somehow about us, at least in the sense that God's unrelenting love is about us or affects us?

In his thick commentary on the parables *Stories with Intent*, Klyne Snodgrass (2008) counsels us against allegorizing or playing "Who's who?" in this parable. *"Should the shepherd be identified with God, Jesus, the disciples, or someone seeking the kingdom?"* he asks. *"And especially, does the parable have Christological implications?"* (p. 106, italics original). In response to such questions, he writes:

Theological allegorizing is out of bounds, but parables generally, and this one specifically, *do* teach theology. Otherwise they would be useless . . . This parable is not saying that God is a shepherd . . . [Instead,] the actions and attitudes portrayed—not the people themselves—mirror the actions and attitude of God . . . The shepherd is not God, Jesus, or anyone else, and the sheep is not a person or group. These figures reside in and stay in the story. Certainly the . . . wilderness and the friends do not "stand for something." At the same time, images selected for stories are not chosen at random; they are specifically chosen to set off resonances, and reference to a shepherd and sheep would bring to mind the OT use of these images for God, leaders, and hope for God's people. (p. 107)

The line that Snodgrass is asking us to walk here is a thin one—against allegorizing and speculating about particular characters but in support of searching out theological meaning, relevance, and human resonance.

But he and other experts invariably and, in my view, inevitably walk this fine line only fitfully, unevenly. Joel B. Green (1997), for example, agrees that the parable is "fundamentally about God, [its] aim to lay bare the nature of the divine response to the recovery of the lost," and Green's convincing reading here would seem to pass the test as an appropriate search for theological meaning and relevance. But Green is equally comfortable saying that Jesus is asking "his audience to identify with a shepherd" (p. 574) or with referring to the "toll collectors and sinners" with whom Jesus eats as the parable's lost sheep (p. 569).

All of this is to say that while caution is in order in our interpretation and use of this or any biblical image or text—none of us aspires to be charged with promoting lone external hierarchical authority or with cavorting with sheep in ministry, or with inserting oneself narcissistically into the biblical text in exegesis—it is always also the case that all of our words about God, even at their most abstract or esoteric or philosophical, and even the Bible's own words, are inevitably also words about *us*; they cannot *not* be about us, specifically because they are always *our* words, necessarily *human* words employing *human* languages to pose *human* questions at some level about whether God has regard for us, about whether you and I are a source of delight to the Source of our delight.

All theologians must read and write and say their words about God, including my words here, without assurance that any is airtight or foolproof or the last word. We can only hope that God is more touched and amused than irritated by them. If at this seminary we are especially vulnerable to finding ourselves lost and are even more confused than we seem, this may be because we are trying to learn to live here without absolute foundations for the things of which we speak. There are simply no unassailable guarantees for our sorts of interests and concerns. We swim here instead in the deep end of the pool, trying to keep afloat in a sea of *faith* (see Martin, 2006, pp. 181–85; Dykstra et al., 2007, pp. 69–70). Every word about God is a human word. Every parable about God is a parable about us, about you and me.

It is not uncontroversial, even to me, to nominate this too rural, too hard, too soft, too individualistic, too *whatever* parable as the most important word about God—and therefore about ourselves—that we could say to ourselves and to one another in the years we are privileged to share here together. But at those not infrequent moments when you find yourself wondering on what planet you have landed when finding yourself lost on Planet Princeton, I would covet your clinging to the mere eighty-nine words (in the Greek) that constitute this parable—memorizing them, tattooing them on some discrete body part, saying them to yourself over and over again— *"Which one of you, having a hundred sheep and losing one of them, does not leave the ninety-nine in the wilderness and go after the one that is lost until he finds it? When he has found it, he lays it on his shoulders and rejoices. And when he comes home, he calls together his friends and neighbors, saying to them, 'Rejoice with me, for I have found my sheep that was lost'"* (Luke 15:1–7)—saying these words about God and about us again and again as a way to restore your equilibrium and reclaim your confidence, in the way of the Dinky, as the little engine that could; remembering again and again Jesus' story of the searching shepherd and one lost sheep just may, like the Wawa, help get you through the night.

Urbane Shepherds

Granted, it is a rural parable. Having come myself, however, from rural roots but by now somewhat adept at faking urbanity, I can tell you that rural and urban (and urbane) people share many things in common—among them a sense that they are all similarly different, all plenty complex, and even more confused than they seem.

Consider, for example, the best-known shepherds in recent memory, who, though fictional and living in an era and region of the country that inexorably consigned their story to tragedy, managed to catch up the rest of the nation and much of the world in their plight. I'm thinking, of course, of Ennis Del Mar and Jack Twist, those young Wyoming shepherds finding themselves lost on Brokeback Mountain in the summer of 1963. Brought to life by Annie Proulx (2003) in her short story in the *New Yorker* in 1997, a prophetic full year before that other Wyoming Shepard's—Matthew Shepard's—murder there, and later by the Ang Lee (2005) film, Jack and Ennis found that after a night on the mountain sharing a bedroll for warmth, they, in Proulx's understated words, "deepened their intimacy considerably" (p. 261). The story unfolds as their lives and loves unravel for another twenty years, mostly apart from one another but sometimes reunited in the mountains, until near the fateful end when Jack cries out in anguish, "You're too much for me, Ennis . . . I wish I knew how to quit you." As it turns out, some thugs with a tire iron help him find a way (p. 278).

Too rural for the modern mind and church, the shepherd and one lost sheep? Given recent disputes within the church, the artistry and tragedy of Proulx's and Lee's shepherds somehow suggest a vocation remarkably current and suitably complex for shaping our discourse about God.

The Shepherd Is the Sheep

What, then, of charges that this parable can "subtly but powerfully convey the idea of the superiority of the pastor over [the] sheep" (Wise, 1966, p. 2) or that it dangerously promotes "lone external hierarchical authority" (Stevenson-Moessner, 1991, p. 201)? These indictments, if sustained, would provide reason enough for rejecting pastoral imagery for informing Christian ministry and faith. But I find inculcated here no such attitude of superiority or hierarchy. To the contrary, the shepherd and sheep in Jesus' parable appear to share a similar lot and unenviable plight. Both are bewildered creatures of low status, if not overtly despised then at least marginalized and ignored: shepherding was considered a vile and religiously forbidden profession in Jesus' day (Jeremias, 1969, pp. 302–12; Scott, 1989, pp. 405, 413; Reid, 2000, p. 184) and, from what I hear, is little esteemed even today; indeed both shepherd and sheep find themselves in a predicament not of their own choosing. However righteous the shepherd may be, I hear flying all manner of expletives in this parable. Sheep and shepherd alike, and not just in the sexual ambiguity they share—for sheep, it turns out, like Jack and Ennis, are famously ambisexual (Dykstra, 2009, pp. 588–90; see also Roughgarden, 2004, pp. 137–42, on the bisexuality of sheep)—sheep and

shepherd alike are multifaceted beings all too familiar with finding themselves lost. As rural and urban persons share a good deal in common, so,
too, to my mind, do shepherd and sheep.

This prospect becomes especially clear to me in a pastoral sense in another parable of sorts about another shepherd, this one nonfictional, who
though counting millions among his flock remained singularly attentive to
the importance of the one, who seemed always to identify with the one—a
shepherd viscerally attuned to the only serious form of the religious question today: *Does God have regard for me?*

The shepherd is Mister Rogers, Fred Rogers, of the children's television program *Mister Rogers' Neighborhood*. Mister Rogers, you may recall,
was a Presbyterian minister who, along with Martin Luther King Jr., likely
comes closest to having attained the status of Protestant sainthood in this
country. Recently on *Weekend Edition*, National Public Radio host Diane
Rehm (2009), reflecting back on her thirty years of conducting NPR interviews with "Nobel laureates and novelists, Supreme Court justices and
presidential candidates," said that "one interview will always stay with her:
'I'll never forget talking with Mister Rogers.'" She spoke of her time with
him just three months before his death in 2003. Others who interviewed
him expressed similar sentiments (Madigan 2006).

In a profile of Mister Rogers published in *Esquire* magazine in 1998,
journalist Tom Junod (1998) describes a visit by Mister Rogers, who lived
in Pittsburgh, to a fourteen-year-old boy who lived in California. The boy
was born with a severe form of cerebral palsy, a disorder of the brain that
interferes not with thinking but sometimes with walking and even talking.
The boy had been abused as a child by caretakers who led him to believe
that he himself was responsible for his condition. Junod writes that now, as
a teenager, the boy "would get so mad at himself that he would hit himself,
hard, with his own fists and tell his mother, on the computer he used for a
mouth, that he didn't want to live anymore, for he was sure that God didn't
like what was inside him any more than he did" (Junod, 1998).

But the boy had always loved Mister Rogers and even at fourteen
"watched the *Neighborhood* whenever it was on." The boy's mother, in
fact, believed that it was Mister Rogers who was keeping her son alive.
She wished that her son could meet him in person—though, since they
lived across the country and the severity of her son's disability prevented
him from traveling, she assumed this would never happen. But then she
"learned through a special foundation designed to help children like her

son that Mister Rogers was coming to California and that after he visited a gorilla named Koko, he was coming to meet her son." Junod (1998) writes:

> At first, the boy was made very nervous by the thought that Mister Rogers was visiting him. He was so nervous, in fact, that when Mister Rogers did visit, he got mad at himself and began hating himself and hitting himself, and his mother had to take him to another room and talk to him. Mister Rogers didn't leave, though. He wanted something from the boy, and Mister Rogers never leaves when he wants something from somebody. He just waited patiently; and when the boy came back, Mister Rogers talked to him, and then he made his request. He said, "I would like you to do something for me. Would you do something for me?" On his computer, the boy answered yes, of course, he would do anything for Mister Rogers, so then Mister Rogers said, "I would like you to pray for me. Will you pray for me?" And now the boy didn't know how to respond. He was thunderstruck. Thunderstruck means that you can't talk, because something has happened that's as sudden and miraculous and maybe as scary as a bolt of lightning, and all you can do is listen to the rumble. The boy was thunderstruck because nobody had ever asked him for something like that, ever. The boy had always been prayed for. The boy had always been the object of prayer, and now he was being asked to pray for Mister Rogers, and although at first he didn't know if he could do it, he said he would, he said he'd try, and ever since then he keeps Mister Rogers in his prayers and doesn't talk about wanting to die anymore, because he figures Mister Rogers is close to God, and if Mister Rogers likes him, that must mean that God likes him, too.

The journalist, shadowing Mister Rogers for the magazine profile, said that when he heard about this story, he complimented Mister Rogers "for being so smart—for knowing that asking the boy for his prayers would make the boy feel better about himself," which of course it must have done. But Mister Rogers, Junod writes, "responded by looking at me first with puzzlement and then with surprise. 'Oh, heavens no, Tom! I didn't ask him for his prayers for him; I asked for me. I asked him because I think that anyone who has gone through challenges like that must be very close to God. I asked him because I wanted his intercession'" (Junod, 1998).

Who in this encounter is shepherd? Who is sheep? We're pretty sure we know as the story opens, but by the end it is not altogether clear. Who is shepherd? Who is sheep? Mr. Rogers is. The fourteen-year-old boy is. His mother is, too. You are. I am. Even Jesus, the teller of *his* shepherding tale:

"You, Lord, are both Lamb and Shepherd. / You, Lord, are both prince and slave" (Dunstan, 1991), we sang hauntingly a few moments ago—the Lamb of God who takes away the sins of the world, the Shepherd of the flock who searches out the one and lifts meager odds that God has regard for us.

To be sure, Mister Rogers, the boy, his mother, and a host of others involved in making provision behind the scenes each plays a distinctive role in this meeting; each has a different task to perform. The shepherd and the sheep here, to borrow some comments of Erik H. Erikson (1981) on Luke 15, "can find themselves and one another only by gaining their own identity in the very fulfillment of their intergenerational roles" (p. 356). Equally apparent, however, is that we discover in Mister Rogers's solicitous wisdom and the boy's audacious faith a shared yearning, a similar complexity, a familiar confusion. How often as faculty we are aware of finding in our students not just our spiritual but, more disconcerting, our intellectual superiors (though, as Erikson helpfully clarifies, we faculty still get to assign the grades).

Far from exhibiting a dangerous form of lone external hierarchical authority, Mister Rogers's plea for the boy's intercession makes me think that, however important our differentiated roles, we shepherds and we sheep share much in common here in the Neighborhood, here on Brokeback Mountain, here on Planet Princeton, here in the kingdom of God. In attending when we can and must to the one over the many—to the individual, to the particular, to the singular, to the lost, to the special, to the marginal in the other *and in ourselves*—we discover not superiority and hierarchy but our only hope for "mutuality without coercion" (Jolly, 2009, p. 101).

What Is Most Personal Is Most General

In perhaps the best-known autobiographical essay from his book *On Becoming a Person*, another distinguished Mister Rogers, this one Carl R. Rogers (1961), who despite the disparagement by Alastair V. Campbell (1981) noted earlier became perhaps the most influential psychotherapist of the twentieth century, reflects on his most important lessons from life. Rogers (1961) writes:

> Somewhere here I want to bring in a learning which has been most rewarding, because it makes me feel so deeply akin to others. I can word it this way. *What is most personal is most general.* There have

been times when in talking with students or staff, or in my writing, I have expressed myself in ways so personal that I have felt I
was expressing an attitude which it was probable no one else could
understand, because it was so uniquely my own . . . In these instances I have almost invariably found that the very feeling which
has seemed to me most private, most personal, and hence most
incomprehensible by others, has turned out to be an expression
for which there is a resonance in many other people. It has led
me to believe that what is most personal and unique in each one
of us is probably the very element which would, if it were shared
or expressed, speak most deeply to others. This has helped me to
understand artists and poets as people who have dared to express
the unique in themselves. (p. 26; italics original)

Artists, poets, and, wouldn't we aspire to add, *seminarians, ministers,* and
theologians, too? People who have dared to express the unique in themselves not as a way to avoid community or context, not in order to live
in isolation in the backwoods of Idaho, but to feel deeply akin to others;
to beautify and beatify community and context; to build, encourage, and
delight in it?

What is most personal is most general. Despite all those words over in
the seminary libraries, not everything about God that *can* be said *has* been
said, for the world still awaits *your* truths, *your* parables, *your* experiences
of searching for, and being found by, our living Lord; the lyrical voice of
the *one* still needs to be heard amid the chorus of the *many.* No shepherd
besides you can think those thoughts; no sheep but you can bleat those
words. That is because, as I heard another psychotherapist, Bill O'Hanlon
(2009), quip, "You are unique, just like everyone else."

Students and faculty, finding themselves lost in confusion and grief,
spontaneously gathered in this room on the morning of September 11,
2001, on hearing of the attacks on New York City and Washington, even as
they had spontaneously gathered in this same room on that Holy Saturday
in April of 1865 on hearing of the death of Abraham Lincoln. So, now, it
is our turn to gather here, even more confused than we seem, rural and
urban, shepherds and sheep, searching and hoping to find, lost and hoping
to be found.

2

Zombie Alleluias

Learning to Live in the Space between Worlds

In an essay titled "On What is Fundamental," Adam Phillips (2010) grapples with one of the most perplexing, even threatening, dilemmas of our day, that of how we might respond in the face of political or religious fundamentalisms, especially extremist versions that threaten violence and destruction to those of differing beliefs. "If it is integral to people's belief that they should destroy you," he asks, "what do you say to them; or, rather more realistically, what do you do with them?" (p. 61).

Phillips's question is an important one to attempt to address, given the anxieties of so many concerning the rise of global fundamentalisms. In deciding to devote some thought to trying to answer it, however, I should have taken a clue from Phillips's essay, in that, in the end, he himself does not answer his own question.

But in trying, and in not quite succeeding, to find its answer, I have become able to name what are for me some important truths about fundamentalism. First and foremost, after initially hoping to find a coherent response to concerns linked to fundamentalism, I realized that the notion that there may be a single, dramatic, or "fundamental" response to phenomena as widespread and complex as these is, of course, a fundamentalist assumption. Fundamentalists, it must say somewhere in the Bible, will always be with you.

As important, I learned that not only will fundamentalists somehow always be with you, with us, but they will always be *in* you, *in* us, as well. I have come to realize that in many ways I too am a fundamentalist. At least part of how we might confront and perhaps alleviate some of the mischief that fundamentalist religious and political movements are generating all around us is by coming to recognize something of our own inner fundamentalists, coming to understand and accept the fundamentalist within, especially as a path to garnering greater empathy with fundamentalist individuals, communities, and movements. I do not assume that empathy alone will be enough to eliminate threats of violence linked to extreme forms of fundamentalism (see Juergensmeyer 2003). But empathy is, I propose, one of the more promising points at which to start.

In trying to come to acknowledge and more fully accept aspects of my own fundamentalist self, I have also sought to consider ways that I, over the span of my life, have been able to change my mind about deeply held convictions—to change meaningful beliefs, views, ideals, and practices in what sometimes felt to be significant ways. I would invite readers, too, to use these moments to reflect on what or, more likely, on *who* has helped pave the way for these kinds of important changes in their lives as well.

Zombies "R" Us

Near the very end of a recent semester, one of my seminary students, taking his first course in pastoral care in the last semester of the final year of his Master of Divinity program and just moments before we were to take our midmorning class break, defiantly declared to his fellow students and me, "I *entered* Princeton Seminary as a fundamentalist, and I'm *leaving* Princeton Seminary as a fundamentalist." He said this with such fundamentalist conviction that I was tempted to believe him.

His words struck me as something of a direct challenge to the course, to me, and perhaps to whatever was the specific subject matter we were discussing that day. It was time for a break. Students had to get a drink of water and stretch their legs. I had to make a split-second decision about whether to respond and, if so, how.

I decided to seize the moment, hoping it might become somehow a teachable one, though I had considerable doubts. How does a moment become teachable for a student proud of the fact that he had spent the past three years resisting being taught something? As is the way with such exchanges, I have been thinking in the time since then about what I did and did not say in response, and what I wished I had said. I have wondered too about what others, especially those with years of experience in Christian ministry, would want to tell, or would have wanted me to tell, this student. His assertion reminded me that there are fundamentalists around us. What I ended up telling him, and more to the point, is that there are also fundamentalists within us: Fundamentalists "R" Us.

Some time ago I asked a friend who is a university chaplain if he wanted to see the blockbuster zombie movie *World War Z* (Forster, 2013), which stars Brad Pitt as chief zombie fighter, a movie I knew neither of our wives would want to see. My friend is usually open to seeing most any film, so I was surprised this time when he turned me down, saying, "No, I work with zombies all day long. It would be too depressing to have to pay good money to see them take over the world."

I understood all too well his reply. He didn't have to elaborate. I knew he was not talking about his students so much as those undead coworkers the purpose of whose lives appears to be generating unending forms or requesting still another report, and who threaten us all with their chaos.

But the fact that I could readily identify with what my friend was saying made it all the more urgent for me to see the movie, for I wanted to know what Brad Pitt would do to fight back, to save the day, to free the world from zombie control. Maybe his skill set would transfer to facing my own institution's zombies. I needed some ammunition, some insight. I hoped he wouldn't let me down.

Zombies are everywhere these days—and not just zombies, but also vampires, werewolves, and other such creatures of the night. Every other book in the young adult fiction section of the local bookstore features apocalyptic creatures and dystopian landscapes. I once asked one of the most prominent such authors, who also heads one of the nation's largest children's publishing houses, whether writers in the genre of young adult fiction feel any responsibility in their books to offer adolescent readers hope for the future, to guard them from despair. He looked at me as if I were a zombie. "No, of course not," he replied. "The only thing that distinguishes young adult from adult fiction is that the protagonists are teenagers" (see also Greenfield, 2012).

Shortly after seeing *World War Z*, I took my daughters, who were ten and fourteen at the time, to a newly released Percy Jackson movie (Freudenthal, 2013), targeted mostly at middle-school youth. Zombies showed up in it, too, though these were entirely harmless if not quite friendly.

But not the zombies of *World War Z*. One of the great achievements of this film is that its zombies are never ironic or campy but are instead truly terrifying. Their only purpose in their quite purpose-driven lives is to devour human flesh.

Max Brooks (2006a), author of the book *World War Z* on which the movie was based, says of zombies:

> They scare me more than any other fictional creature out there because they break all the rules . . . Zombies don't act like a predator; they act like a virus, and that is the core of my terror. A predator is intelligent by nature, and knows not to overhunt its feeding ground. A virus will just continue to spread, infect, and consume, no matter what happens. It's the mindlessness behind it. (quoted in Eton, 2006)

"The lack of rational thought has always scared me when it came to zombies," Brooks (2006b) says, "the idea that there is no middle ground . . . Any kind of mindless extremism scares me, and we're living in some pretty extreme times."

Zombies, in other words, are fundamentalists. They are extremists. There is no negotiating, no horse trading, no compromising, no recognition or tolerance of the other with them. Thus, Brooks believes, zombies become a social metaphor for government ineptitude and Orwellian tactics, for corporate corruption and science deniers, for religious and political fundamentalisms flourishing everywhere today. Zombies appear in our collective cultural life to allow us to deal with our anxieties about the end of the world. They are trying to help us cope. They signify our fears.

On Living, Psychologically Speaking, Beyond Our Means

There is a good deal of agreement among psychologists of religion concerning the psychological components of the fundamentalist, which is to say a zombie-like, mind. What makes for a fundamentalist way of thinking? In the introductory chapter of their book *The Fundamentalist Mindset: Psychological Perspectives on Religion, Violence, and History*, Charles B. Strozier and Katherine A. Boyd (Strozier et al., 2010) suggest that

> the fundamentalist mindset, wherever it occurs, is composed of distinct characteristics, including dualistic thinking; paranoia and rage in a group context; an apocalyptic orientation that incorporates distinct perspectives on time, death, and violence; a

relationship to charismatic leadership; and a totalized conversion experience . . . One also returns frequently in the literature to psychological themes of shame and humiliation, to the need for simplified meanings, and most of all for the absolutist and totalized way things get structured in the fundamentalist mindset. (pp. 11–12)

In *The Battle for God*, Karen Armstrong (2000, p. xiii; cited in Phillips, 2010, pp. 72–73) says that fundamentalism is

a reaction against the scientific and secular culture that first appeared in the West, but which has since taken root in other parts of the world. The West has developed an entirely unprecedented and wholly different type of civilization, so the religious response to it has been unique. The fundamentalist movements that have evolved in our own day have a symbiotic relationship with modernity. They may reject the scientific rationalism of the West, but they cannot escape it. Western civilization has changed the world. Nothing—including religion—can ever be the same again.

Above all, psychologists who study fundamentalism point to dualistic thinking as its central aspect—to such a degree, according to Strozier and Boyd (2010, p. 14), that "the centrality of binary oppositions defines the fundamentalist mindset." Quoting Robert M. Young, they suggest that "dualistic thinking causes one to 'see others in very partial terms—as part-objects,' such that fundamentalists 'lose the ability to imagine the inner humanity of others'" (see also Young, 2002, pp. 210–11). Fundamentalists, in this view, have a difficult time experiencing empathy. Fundamentalism becomes an exercise in failed empathy, in lacking the capacity to imagine others' inner lives.

Returning, then, to the opening question posed by Phillips (2010, p. 61)—"If it is integral to people's belief that they should destroy you, what do you say to them; or, rather more realistically, what do you do with them?"—how might we respond in the face of political or religious fundamentalisms, especially extremist versions that threaten violence and destruction to those of differing beliefs? Is it possible to resist fundamentalists without becoming one yourself? Indeed, Phillips wonders, might not one's very claims to tolerance serve to perpetuate fundamentalist projects, wherein "religious moderates, by being moderate, appease religious fanatics and by so doing allow them to flourish"? He poses what he calls "the perennial post-enlightenment question": "What is it to adequately oppose scriptural literalism and the religious violence it often entails? Can we avoid violating our core beliefs in the ways we defend them?" (p. 61). Can religious moderates and political democracies manage to contain the bullies without bullying in return?

Phillips's questions are not merely academic or abstract but penetrate to the anxieties that increasingly trouble individuals, churches, even nations. Ecumenical pastors in Geneva gowns look with no little envy on what appears to be the fervent growth of fundamentalist churches, whose ministers lead worship in jeans and T-shirts in sound-stage chancels energized by rock bands. (Fundamentalists who oppose modern culture tend to use the culture's latest technologies to convey their message; see Lifton, 1993, pp. 164–66, 183–84.) But ecumenical types also look with suspicion on smooth certainties about the Bible and literalism in biblical reading among fundamentalists. Ecumenical Christians are mindful of the human fallout from fundamentalists' confidence about who are "sheep" and who are "goats" (Matt 25:32–33), and skeptical of fundamentalists' self-assurance about all that God intends for the world.

Beyond the walls of churches, citizens of the West live in the wake of 9/11 with low-grade anxiety over an underlying threat of religiously sanctioned violence (Juergensmeyer, 2003, pp. 3–15, 127–28, 188–89), even as America's recent perpetual wars or casual concession to government surveillance suggest evidence of a tendency for overreaction on the one hand, or expedient compliance on the other.

In his book *Why Teach? In Defense of a Real Education*, Mark Edmundson (2013), a literature professor at the University of Virginia, comments on the frenetic activities of his undergraduate students, who jet around the globe to accumulate exotic experiences, a lifestyle pace he attributes to anxiety in the wake of the "near-American Apocalypse" of September 11, 2001. "No one," he says,

> believes that the whole [American] edifice is likely to topple down around us soon. But everyone now lives with the knowledge that today, tomorrow, next week, we can suffer an event that will change everything drastically. A dirty bomb in the middle of a great city, poison wafting in sweet-smelling clouds through a subway system, a water supply tainted . . . Tomorrow the deck may be shuffled and recut by the devil's hand. So what shall we do now? (pp. 34–35)

The answer of Edmundson's students, it strikes him, appears to be,

Live, live, before the bombs go off in San Francisco or the water goes vile in New York . . . On that bad day there will be, at the very least, the start of a comprehensive *closing down*. There will be no more free travel, no more easy money, and much less loose talk . . . There's a humane hunger to my students' hustle for more life—but I think it's possible that down below bubbles a fear. Do it now, for later may be too late. (2013, p. 35, italics original)

How, then, in the face of unrelenting anxieties, are ecumenical Christians who pride themselves on tolerance, and political democrats confronting theocratic reactions to anxiety at home and abroad, to respond in the face of religious and political fundamentalisms? Is it possible, Phillips (2010, p. 61) wonders, to "avoid violating our core beliefs in the ways we defend them? If it is integral to people's belief that they should destroy you, what do you say to them; what do you do with them?"

As I have noted, Phillips never finally answers his perhaps unanswerable questions. He hints, however, that one important way to begin addressing them is to recognize and pay closer attention to those fundamentalists we harbor within. Everyone is a fundamentalist about *something*, Phillips (2010) asserts, and "one of the ways we recognize the fundamental things when they turn up in conversation is that people tend to lose their composure when they talk about them":

An obvious rule of thumb would be: people become violent, lose their civility, when something that is fundamental to them is felt to be under threat. And what psychoanalysis adds to this is that fundamental things sometimes get displaced . . . ; we can't be as sure as we would like to be that we always know what we are arguing about. (pp. 49–50)

We are all fundamentalists, all fanatics, all literalists about some sacred or secular scripture or another, Phillips is saying, even those of us whose fundamental "something" or "scripture" may be the importance of valuing human differences or of tolerating the other. Tolerance fundamentalists readily grow intolerant of the intolerance of others. Thus, our beliefs—even the religious and political beliefs of those whose fundamental quest may be for terms of coexistence and toleration of difference, and whose fundamental sensitivities reflect a deep aversion to fundamentalism—get linked to violence. "We kill people to defend our virtues, not our vices," Phillips (2010, p. 50) observes; "People are prepared to die and kill for other . . .

people's sentences" (p. 55). Best to begin by acknowledging this part of who we are, to become attuned to the fundamentalists found within.

Freud (1923a, pp. 17ff.) called the original fundamentalist of the human soul the "id" or "not-I," describing it as "a chaos, a cauldron full of seething excitations" (1933a, p. 65) and insistent desires, which includes animalistic drives that press for biological survival and sensory pleasure within persons. Freud (1923a, pp. 22, 32–33) called the second inner fundamentalist the "superego" or "above-I," an agency of the self that includes, in part, an individual's inner moral compass or conscience but also the repository for strictures on the child both from its parents and from accumulating demands of the larger social world. The superego demands of the maturing child rigid compliance to those strictures.

Both the id and the superego, Phillips (2010, p. 61) notes, are "without skepticism about their own commitments." They are that tiny fundamentalist demon and equally ruthless little angel who, though usually unconscious and therefore furtive, perch one atop each shoulder and whisper in one's ears of unrelenting personal passions and of severe self-condemnation. "The 'drives' of the id are, in this picture, the fundamental promptings of our being, the superego the fundamental promptings of our being in culture," Phillips (2010, pp. 62–63) observes.

Everyone is a fundamentalist about something, each person harboring these two relentless fundamentalists—id and superego—within. But because these inner fundamentalists are largely unconscious, hidden even from the self, it becomes easy to lose track of them, repress them, or express them in symptomatic ways not usually recognized as such. *It therefore becomes almost impossible to voice or speak with any coherence of the things that matter most to us* (Phillips, 2010, pp. 77–78). When we respond intolerantly to the intolerant in our quest for tolerance, as perhaps we must, we cannot be as sure as we would like to be, Freud is saying, that we know precisely what we are arguing about. It may have very little to do with a desire for tolerance at all.

In an essay written a century ago, Freud (1915, p. 174) reflects on the disillusionment of his fellow Austrians and the citizens of other so-called advanced nations at the epicenter of World War I. Their disillusionment sprang, he says, from seeing how quickly those who espoused tolerance and civility could morph into barbarians who unleashed a level of brutality previously "considered irreconcilable with their level of civilization." Freud himself, however, is not among those disillusioned by his neighbors' and nation's sudden shift to cruelty in the war. He couldn't be disillusioned by incivility, he says, because he held so few illusions about civility to begin with. You can't be *dis*illusioned unless you've first been *illusioned.*

From years of his own relentless internal self-scrutiny and from hearing secrets entrusted to him by patients in the privacy of the psychoanalytic hour, Freud (1929, pp. 38–39) had come to know much about unsanctioned sexual desires and murderous aggression usually masked by a veneer of civilized morality. Modern civilization insists that we wear these masks, reinforcing a constant state of psychological hypocrisy and illusion. We cannot show ourselves, we cannot even *know* ourselves, as we really are. These social masks are necessary for modern civilization to function, to be sure, Freud realizes, but we pay a high psychological price as individuals for wearing them. Modern civilization presses us to live, "psychologically speaking, beyond [our] means," Freud (1915, p. 178) says. We have few reserves in our psychological bank accounts, living instead on a precarious line of emotional credit. Then at times, as with the enormous stress of wartime, this disquieting psychological system breaks down. The anxiety and tension erupt, the masks of civility fall away, and our moral uprightness gets exposed as illusory.

Modern citizens are pressured to live beyond their psychological means, compelled to maintain high monthly balances on their emotional credit cards: "One in ten Americans now takes an anti-depressant medication; among women in their forties and fifties, the figure is one in four," *The New York Times* reports (Rabin, 2013). Nearly three in ten Americans experience clinical levels of anxiety. More than that, writes Daniel Smith (2012) in his personal memoir of anxiety *Monkey Mind*, anxiety is

> a universal and insoluble feature of modern life. Everyone has it; everyone must deal with it . . . The corollary to this is that everyone's anxiety is different, shot through with idiosyncratic concerns and confusions . . . . Anxiety compels a person to think, but it is the type of thinking that gives thinking a bad name: solipsistic, self-eviscerating, unremitting, vicious. (p. 4)

Anxiety is a universal and insoluble feature of modern life. Freud's reflections grow only timelier a century after World War I. As the bank accounts of individuals' souls run low, their anxieties run high. And even publishers of children's books express little concern to guard young people from despair.

It is a complex world. We are complex persons. There is so much more to each of us than meets the eye, tensions and contradictions within and without. It is not difficult, given these circumstances, to understand the appeal of various fundamentalisms that infect and consume like a virus in our collective religious and political life. One can appreciate the hypnotic allure of extremism, the desire to forsake complexity and cling to charismatic certainty, the magnetic draw of intolerance toward those who differ from oneself or one's identified group. One can understand zombie-like temptations to break all the rules or to live with devastating clarity. Anxiety is all around. We are living beyond our means, the zombies closing in.

The Ecumenical Self

But we are not, according to Freud, left completely at the mercies of our inner fundamentalists, of the *id* or "not-I" and of the *superego* or "above-I." There is a third inner agency, Freud recognized, namely, the *ego* or, more simply, the *I*, that attempts to negotiate between those inner agencies without skepticism about their commitments.

One way to understand the ego is as the sole agency of the self that is not a scriptural literalist, the agency that, unlike one's inner fundamentalists and unlike those fundamentalists one meets on the street, does not always know in advance exactly what it wants or have at the ready an instant answer for each of life's perplexities. Instead, the *I* is that voice within every individual willing to explore possible alternatives, seeking to soften hardened binaries, negotiating common ground between clashing worlds (see Phillips, 2010, p. 71; Dykstra, 2001, pp. 86–88).

The *ego* or *I* in this understanding is a beleaguered but invaluable referee, an inner progressive voice even in the outwardly most conservative of persons, including, I presume, in my fundamentalist former student. The ego patiently raises its hand in the back of the room in order to get a word in edgewise. The ego, Phillips (2010, p. 63) suggests, is "an experiment in imagining, in describing what in ourselves may be available to manage the prevailing forms of fundamentalism in which we live." The ego, in other words, is "a democrat in a world of fascists" (p. 68).

While Freud was not optimistic concerning the ego's capacities to manage the self's inner fundamentalists, neither did he believe that individuals are left completely bereft in this regard. The ego, rather, is the rider "obliged to guide [the horse]" in the direction the *horse* wants to go (Freud, 1923a, p. 19; Phillips, 2010, p. 63).

Erik H. Erikson (1968), in *Identity, Youth, and Crisis*, builds on Freud's understanding of the ego and the complex nature of the self. The ego or *I* for Erikson, is one's sense of holding together many selves experienced within. What we commonly refer to when we say "I" is, for Erikson, a collection of many inner experiences, of many different internal "selves." The *I* is thus a *composite* Self:

> What the "I" reflects on when it sees or contemplates the body, the personality, and the roles to which it is attached for life—not knowing where it was before or will be after—are the various selves which make up our composite Self. There are constant and often shocklike transitions between these selves: consider the nude body self in the dark or suddenly exposed in the light; consider the clothed self among friends or in the company of higher-ups or lower-downs; consider the just awakened drowsy self or the one stepping refreshed out of the surf or the one overcome by retching and fainting; the body self in sexual excitement or in a rage; the competent self and the impotent one; the one on horseback, the one in the dentist's chair, and the one chained and tortured—by men who also say "I." It takes, indeed, a healthy personality for the "I" to be able to speak out of all of these conditions in such a way that at any given moment it can testify to a reasonably coherent Self. (p. 217)

Donald Capps (2014a, pp. 141–67), in a chapter titled "Happy Spirits and Grumpy Souls" on the subject of mood changes in older adulthood, draws on Erikson's (1968) notion of the composite Self. He rechristens it the *ecumenical self* and emphasizes its aspects or constituencies—the melancholy self as one prominent example—that endure over a longer period of time than those described above by Erikson (see also Capps, 2013, pp. xiii, 5). Capps (2014a, pp. 146–64) considers Walt Disney's 1937 film version of the Grimm brothers' fairy tale "Snow White and the Seven Dwarfs" (Hand, 1937) in relation to the mood changes that often lead older adult men, in the popular imagination, to be characterized as grumpy ("Get off my lawn!"). He therefore zeroes in especially on the two dwarfs in *Snow White* whom Disney named Happy and Grumpy.

Capps offers a measured endorsement of the popular view of older men as increasingly prone to unpleasant moods, but with a caveat, noting that in the fairy tale Grumpy has good reason to be unhappy. Why?

Because his natural disposition alerts him "to the fact that things can go seriously wrong in the world he inhabits" (Capps, 2014a, p. 159), especially in this case if a strange woman shows up unbidden at one's door, presumes to begin tidying one's house, and, more ominously, claims to be a princess condemned by a wicked queen. Grumpy rightly perceives that Snow White—and he and his fellow dwarfs—are in imminent danger. Whereas Grumpy's fellow dwarf, Happy, approaches life by simply accepting things at face value, as they are or appear to be, Grumpy envisions a more ominous, but imminently possible, future. In the case of Snow White and the danger her presence in the cottage portends for all who live there, Grumpy's intuitions, of course, prove to be astute. Yes, older adult men may be prone to mood changes associated with grumpiness, Capps suggests, but they have good reason to be grumpy.

But even as he recognizes an increasing tendency toward grumpiness in the lives of older adult men, he acknowledges that he would have made no such claim if he believed that "grumpy old men are nothing but grumpy souls." Instead," he writes, "I am convinced that Grumpy is only one of the seven dwarfs that inhabit the cottage that I know as myself and, this being the case, he must share the living space with Doc, Happy, Bashful, Sneezy, Sleepy, and Dopey":

> Thus, to invoke Gordon W. Allport's (1950) image of the ecumenical movement in reference to the role of temperament in the formation and maintenance of the religious sentiment, I would want to suggest that the "composite Self" that Erik H. Erikson discusses in *Identity, Youth, and Crisis* is itself an ecumenical body comprised of various selves. (Capps, 2014a, p.162)

Capps further stakes a claim for a unique bond between Happy and Grumpy within an individual's ecumenical self, whereby one's Happy self tries to accept at face value and "to adapt as best he can to the 'wrongness in life,'" even while one's Grumpy self feels "the need to complain or protest and, if possible, to do something about it" (Capps, 2014a, p. 163).

Thus, Freud, Erikson, and Capps variously speak to the complexity and multiplicity of our experiences of self; inner democrats attempt to contain and assuage inner fascists. As Phillips (1994, pp. 48–50) claims, referring to Freud's tripartite division of the soul, "We are always doing at least two things at once, and this can mean that the art of psychotherapy . . . is turning what feel like contradictions—incompatibilities—into paradoxes" (see also Dykstra et al., 2007, pp. 54–55).

Turning Contradictions into Paradoxes

Inner progressive agencies of the self engage, cajole, and compete and seek compromise with, the self's inner fundamentalists. One question that comes to mind in light of the internal multiplicity or ecumenicity of the self is whether ecumenical churches—those churches often referred to, perhaps misleadingly in the face of dwindling memberships, as mainline Protestant—and their ministers and theologies contribute in some small way, within their members and in their surrounding communities and relationships, to the strengthening of the ecumenical self. Do ecumenical churches, ministers, and theologies contribute to the formation of selves less inclined toward dualisms, less enamored of binary oppositions, less rigid, paranoid, apocalyptic, or "undead"? I raise this question mindful of Phillips's (2010, pp. 60–61) countercharge that religious moderates may instead actually *perpetuate* the problems of fundamentalism in their very tolerance of fundamentalists.

How do we seek to incorporate within ourselves and in those entrusted to our care a greater openness to the complexity, multiplicity, or ecumenicity of their inner psychological experience and of their experience of persons and communities around them? How do we soften binary oppositions within us and between us? How in the past have our own minds managed to change, subtly or dramatically, about previously held beliefs and practices? Again, while there are no simple answers to these questions, just as there is none for Phillips's question of how we are to respond to those whose beliefs lead them to seek to destroy us, I offer a few reflections here by way of entering the conversation about how we might learn to live more fully into our ecumenical selves, to live more comfortably in the necessarily uncomfortable space between worlds.

Let me return for a moment to the seminary student who challenged his fellow students and me by saying that he had entered Princeton Seminary as a fundamentalist and was leaving Princeton Seminary as a fundamentalist. I began my attempt to respond to him by trying to identify personally with his conservatism, that is, with his desire to *conserve* something important to him, to *preserve* something fundamental to him. I told him that all of us have aspects of our lives and beliefs that are important for us to protect or conserve, but that it is also the case that even major changes in our beliefs, viewpoints, opinions, or desires over the years follow a surprisingly conservative pattern. Change is a fundamentally conservative process. Even in the most dramatic of changes, much in our lives, indeed almost everything, remains fundamentally unchanged.

I drew this claim from William James's (1907/2003) 1907 book *Pragmatism*. James asks in the book how anyone comes to new opinions, and he concludes that

> the process here is always the same. The individual has a stock of old opinions already, but he meets a new experience that puts them to a strain. Somebody contradicts them; or in a reflective moment he discovers that they contradict each other; or he hears of facts with which they are incompatible; or desires arise in him they cease to satisfy. The result is an inward trouble to which his mind till then had been a stranger, and from which he seeks to escape by modifying his previous mass of opinions. He saves as much of it as he can, for in this matter of belief we are all extreme conservatives. So he tries to change first this opinion, and then that (for they resist change very variously), until at last some new idea comes up which he can graft upon the ancient stock with a minimum of disturbance of the latter . . .
>
> [Even] the most violent revolutions in an individual's beliefs leave most of his old order standing. Time and space, cause and effect, nature and history, and one's own biography remain untouched. New truth is always a go-between, a smoother-over of transitions. It marries old opinion to new fact so as ever to show a minimum of jolt, a maximum of continuity . . . (Even the most ancient truths were themselves once plastic.) . . . [These ancient truths] also mediated between still earlier truths and what in those days were novel observations. Purely objective truth, truth in whose establishment the function of giving human satisfaction in marrying previous parts of experience with new parts played no role whatever, is nowhere to be found. (James, 1907/2003, pp. 26–29)

Changing one's mind about some fundamental conviction, as most every adult has done at some point or another, James is saying, is at once a quite conservative and a simultaneously radical kind of act—*conservative* in the sense that even after the change most everything in one's life continues to remain the same; *radical* in the sense of contributing to the realization that all truths, even the most ancient ones, were at one time malleable and that therefore—the fundamentalist's nightmare—purely objective truth is nowhere to be found.

Another former seminary student of mine is the son of a tall-steeple Baptist minister from a southern state. The student was open about being a gay man on campus at a time not long ago when such candor was not common. He had come out to his conservative parents as a teenager many years earlier. Learning of his sexual orientation was not something they had wanted to hear from him. In the initial aftermath of his revelation, both sides maintained radio silence concerning his sexuality. Eventually, however, Tim decided to make a point of bringing up his orientation, to his parents' discomfort, each time he went home for holidays or school breaks. He refused to allow them to ignore this important part of who he was. His parents remained entrenched in their opposition long past his graduation from the seminary and for years into his first professional position as a nonordained but openly gay youth minister in a working-class Presbyterian congregation, itself not entirely supportive of gay rights, in the urban East. Meanwhile, he began the process of preparing for a day when he might be allowed to be ordained as an "out" gay minister in the Presbyterian Church (U.S.A.).

That day eventually arrived, as that denomination voted to allow the ordination of gay and lesbian persons in 2012. Tim asked his father not only to attend his ordination service but, if he was willing, to offer the customary scriptural charge to the newly ordained minister. To his surprise, his father agreed. Likewise, though such an ordination strained the belief system of the little congregation with which Tim had been working, parishioners nonetheless rallied in their historic role and witness in hosting the ceremony.

A few months after the fact, I received an e-mail from Tim telling of his ordination service. He said, "My father gave the charge, which was truly an amazing moment. For me, it would have been enough if he had simply read the phone book, but he gave a beautiful charge and thanked the church for 'being there for our son when our family was not.' Not an accolade the church often receives, but there were a lot of tears" (personal correspondence, May 6, 2013).

In certain respects, this poignant series of events reflects and underscores William James's claim concerning the ultimately conservative nature of even seemingly dramatic changes of beliefs in an individual's or community's life. Despite the father's gradual, dramatic, and moving change of mind and heart concerning issues surrounding his son's sexual orientation, and despite the anxieties of Tim's little congregation and the recent thawing of historically entrenched ecclesiastical doctrine that for many previous centuries would have disallowed this ordination, almost everything will remain the same in that father's, in that congregation's, and in that denomination's life. As William James indicates, the father's biography, for example, including his hometown; his parents; his previous teachers and mentors; his eye color and tastes in food and clothing; his favorite sports teams, authors, and pastimes; not to mention time and space and the effects of gravity that continue to hold his feet on the ground—all will remain intact for him, as it will for Tim's gracious congregation and for his and other ecumenical Christian denominations that have altered former policies concerning ordination. This is the way it always has been, James says: "Even the most ancient truths were themselves once plastic." But then a bush was seen to be burning but not consumed; then an enslaved people who should not have survived somehow managed to escape through the sea; then a man who should have remained dead appeared to followers who insisted on claiming his resurrection. A new truth had to be woven into the fabric of existing truths, an at once completely conservative and also quite radical prospect and process of "turning what feel like contradictions—incompatibilities—into paradoxes" (Phillips, 1994, p. 50). We are, individually and corporately, persistent yet malleable ecumenical selves and bodies.

Returning then to the earlier case of the seminarian proud to be graduating as a fundamentalist, I somehow wanted to affirm for him that he too, along with his teacher and every one of his future parishioners, was a complex self—fundamentalist and progressive, fascist and democrat—and that he had *nothing* and *everything* to fear as he left our halls for Christian ministry.

Learning to Live in the Space between Worlds

In the months following my conversation with him in class that day, I have found myself reflecting on the ways my own beliefs and practices, even foundational ones, have changed over the years, and how such change, however painful, became possible for me. How is it that one can and sometimes does come to embrace one's own inner contradictions and complexities, to change one's political loyalties, or to allow oneself to think or believe something one did not think or believe before? For me, this embrace of a fuller and more threatening ecumenicity of my inner experience and of my experience of others who seem so different from me, however halting, has come most predictably in *relationships of friendship and love,* and paradoxically in relationships with those who love or accept me *as I already am.* I come to change, in other words, by way of relationships *in which I am not pressed to change.*

Carl R. Rogers (1961), in autobiographical remarks titled "This Is Me" in his most influential book *On Becoming a Person,* said:

> The paradoxical aspect of my experience is that the more I am simply willing to be myself, in all this complexity of life, and the more I am willing to understand and accept the realities in myself and in the other person, the more change seems to be stirred up. It is a very paradoxical thing—that to the degree that each one of us is willing to be himself, then he finds not only himself changing; but he finds that other people to whom he relates are also changing. At least this is a very vivid part of my experience, and one of the deepest things I think I have learned in my personal and professional life. (p. 22)

Grace, which Paul Tillich (1952, pp. 163–67) once likened to *acceptance,* including, I would add, *self-*acceptance, precedes change for Rogers. This is, of course, a very conservative—even fundamental—but concurrently quite radical Protestant notion.

In his book *The Death of Sigmund Freud,* Mark Edmundson (2007, p. 104) suggests that Freud "freed people so that they could bear at first just to glance at their strangest wishes, and then to stare with a spirit of calm toleration and even humor." How did Freud enable his patients to tolerate and even laugh at their inner contradictions? He did this, he said, by means of a therapeutic relationship that involved what clinically he called "transference" but also at one point more simply, in a 1906 letter to Carl Jung, "love": Psychoanalysis, he said, "in essence is a cure through love" (Freud & Jung, 1979, p. 10). The kind of love that accepts one as one already is, without need of change, is a love that finally allows the individual, from time to time, to be able actually to change.

An example of one such change in my own adolescence occurred when it eventually dawned on me, in reading again the Genesis accounts of creation and the fall (3:1–5), that serpents do not talk. This story, I suddenly knew, could not be true! But if serpents do not talk and the story is not true, then about what other things, I wondered, had I also been deceived in church over the years? A process of change that developmental psychologists would recognize as an adolescent's predictable cognitive shift from concrete to formal operational thinking felt instead to me at the time as a quaking of the foundations of my faith. I had been misled, I thought, not, like Eve, by a serpent but, even worse, by the religious traditions I had long trusted and loved.

I went to talk with my minister, a man I held in high esteem. With a great sense of urgency, I ranted about how I had been sold a bill of goods by the church. *Serpents don't talk! It's all a lie!* He listened in complete silence until I had exhausted my tirade. Then in quiet composure he responded with just three words: "It's a myth."

His demeanor was disarming. I was not sure I knew what he meant by "myth." But the fact that he could accept my critical questioning of the Bible and our shared faith without defensiveness, with obvious interest in and care for my concerns, allowed me to begin to grow into a richer new hermeneutic of Scripture and life (and one that, not incidentally, might allow me today to believe again that serpents *can* talk, even as I notice around and within me that zombies can walk). I learned that day, and in many that would follow, that my teachers would not recoil as I grew into a mind and a skin that was more complex, more mature, more faithful to a wider range of my own experience, more *mine*, than what I had once known as a child. Christian faith for me was not going to have to be all-or-nothing, either-or, black-or-white, intellect or feeling, or body or soul. Instead, for better or worse, I was being invited to learn to live in the space between worlds.

Sebastian Moore (2007, p. 30, italics original), a British Benedictine monk, writes: "The Church's task is the huge one, to get the triumph of life over death into non-mythic language, into the triumph of life in you and me over the fear in you and me that is also fear *between* you and me." How shall we accomplish this, with anxiety rampant all around?

For decades, and increasingly often after 9/11, Fred Rogers (2014), the Presbyterian minister beloved for his PBS children's television show *Mister Rogers' Neighborhood*, would tell of a way his mother attempted one such transliteration from the mythic into the mundane, from fear into triumph, in this case by seeking to comfort him as a child in the wake of tragic events that garnered much media attention:

> When I was a boy and I would see scary things in the news, my mother would say to me, "Look for the helpers. You will always find people who are helping." To this day, especially in times of "disaster," I remember my mother's words and I am always comforted

by realizing that there are still so many helpers—so many caring
people in this world.

Rogers's mother sought to protect her son from anxiety and despair by encouraging him to search out a more complex picture of tragedy. She invited
him to enter a more ecumenical space between worlds than that to which,
from sensationalist media reports alone, he might otherwise have been inclined to attend.

In light of Adam Phillips's (2010, p. 61) question that opened this
essay—"If it is integral to people's belief that they should destroy you,
what do you say to them; or, rather more realistically, what do you do with
them?"—and of Sebastian Moore's (2007, p. 30) equally urgent appeal for
Christians to "get the triumph of life over death into non-mythic language,
into the triumph of life in you and me over the fear in you and me that is
also fear *between* you and me"—I have been attempting to speak, however
haltingly, of the therapeutic importance of relationships of love, or what
more specifically we might call *empathy*, by way of response. I know only
too well that a call for empathy amid the onslaught of viral fundamentalisms, within us and without, will appear to be embarrassingly naive as a
means to face relentless anxieties of our times. But empathy strikes me as
a far more powerful instrument for changing the fear within and between
persons into the triumph of life over death among them than at first glance
may be apparent.

In an opinion piece in the *New York Times* published only weeks after
the election as president of Donald Trump, as one timely example, R. Derek
Black (2016), son of the founder of *Stormfront*, the first white nationalist
website, and godson of prominent white nationalist David Duke, tells how
as a college student he came to reject the ideology in which he had been
raised. Growing up in Palm Beach, Florida, immediately across from Donald Trump's Mar-a-Lago estate, Black was elected in 2008, at age nineteen,
to a Palm Beach County Republican committee seat. He "was once considered the bright future of the [white nationalist] movement," noting that Mr.
Trump's presidential campaign comments, beginning with his "Mexican
rapists" speech,

> echoed how I also tapped into less-than-explicit white national-
> ist ideology to reach relatively moderate white Americans. I went
> door-to-door in 2008 talking about how Hispanic immigration
> was overwhelming "American" culture, how black neighborhoods

were hotbeds of crime, and how P.C. culture didn't let us talk about any of it. I won that small election with 60 percent of the vote.

A few years later Black transferred from a community college to a more progressive liberal arts college, where his presence and relative notoriety generated, in his words, "huge controversy." He was startled to find there that others feared him, when previously he had believed he "was only doing what was right and defending those I loved."

Black's views began to change, however, through encounters in which others in the college community voiced "clear and passionate outrage to what I believed" but while also continuing to engage rather than shun him, beginning with an invitation from an Orthodox Jewish student to attend a weekly Shabbat dinner with other students (Saslow, 2016): "Through many talks with devoted and diverse people—those who chose to invite me into their dorms and conversations rather than ostracize me—I began to realize the damage I had done. Ever since, I have been trying to make up for it" (Black, 2016). Black, now a graduate student in medieval studies, asserts that citizens, in the aftermath of Mr. Trump's election, "have a duty to protect those who are threatened by this administration and to win over those who don't recognize the impact of their vote." Given ostracism from his family for his current views, he is likewise aware of the many challenges inherent in such actions (Saslow, 2016). But at its core, he claims, will be a process akin to empathy: "People have approached me looking for a way to change the minds of Trump voters, but I can't offer any magic technique. That kind of persuasion happens in person-to-person interactions and it requires a lot of honest listening on both sides" (Black, 2016).

Here is a second example of the power of empathy amid extremism: On August 20, 2013, Michael Hill, a twenty-year-old man who had not taken his psychiatric medication, walked into McNair Discovery Learning Academy, a school of over eight hundred elementary-age children in Decatur, Georgia, with an AK-47 rifle, five hundred rounds of ammunition, and, in his words, "nothing to live for." He immediately took as a hostage the school's bookkeeper, Antoinette Tuff, who, while fearing for her life, calmly talked with him *as if he were a human being* for twenty-four minutes, their entire conversation recorded on a 9-1-1 emergency line. Her words to Michael during that seemingly endless period of time managed to save not only their lives but those of everyone else in the school. Gary Younge (Aug. 25, 2013), a journalist for the *Guardian*, writes:

"We're not going to hate you," [Tuff] said, referring to [Hill] first as "sir" and later as "sweetie" and "baby." "My pastor, he just started this teaching on anchoring, and how you anchor yourself in the Lord," recalled Tuff, who said she was terrified. "I just sat there and started praying."

And so in between updates with the 911 dispatcher she shared her own travails with Hill, telling him about her divorce and disabled son, all the while reassuring him. "I love you. I'm proud of you. We all go through something in life. You're gonna be OK, Sweetheart. I tried to commit suicide last year after my husband left me." Eventually, while keeping police at a distance, she persuaded him to give up his weapons, lie on the floor, and give himself up.

"If it is integral to people's belief that they should destroy you, what do you say to them?" How do we "get the triumph of life over death into non-mythic language, into the triumph of life in you and me over the fear in you and me that is also fear *between* you and me"? Who will teach us to live in the face of fundamental forces of destruction all around? How do we learn to live into the complexity of our ecumenical selves? Who will help us to live in the space between worlds?

3

Unrepressing the Kingdom

Pastoral Theology as Aesthetic Imagination

Once Jesus was asked by the Pharisees when the kingdom of God was coming, and he answered, "The kingdom of God is not coming with things that can be observed; nor will they say, 'Look, here it is!' or 'There it is!' For, in fact, the kingdom of God is among you."

—LUKE 17:20–21

For forty-three minutes during rush hour on a Friday morning in January of 2007, in the entrance to the busy L'Enfant Plaza subway station in downtown Washington, D.C., Joshua Bell, one of the world's greatest classical violinists, performed six of what he considered to be the most beautiful pieces of music ever written. Dressed in sneakers and jeans, a T-shirt and baseball cap, he was playing a Stradivarius valued at $3.5 million, its case with a few dollars in seed money opened to collect donations from passersby. According to Gene Weingarten (2007), the journalist who had enlisted Bell to stage a social experiment for the *Washington Post*, and whose subsequent front-page article about it garnered a Pulitzer Prize, three days earlier "Bell had filled the house at Boston's stately Symphony Hall, where merely pretty good seats went for $100."

If one were to take great art out of its regular context, would anyone notice? Asked to consider performing in the subway station for what the *Post* envisioned, in Weingarten's words, "as an experiment in context, perceptions and priorities—as well as an unblinking assessment of public taste: In a banal setting at an inconvenient time, would beauty transcend?"—Bell unblinkingly responded, "Sounds like fun." So, opening with "Chaconne" from Bach's Partita No. 2 in D Minor, which Bell called "not just one of the greatest pieces of music ever written, but one of the greatest achievements of any man in history," he proceeded to play to the passing rush hour crowd, all of this recorded on hidden cameras placed around the subway entrance.

It took three minutes into the first piece before even a minor breakthrough took place: one man among the sixty-three people who had already walked by "altered his gait for a split second, turning his head to notice that there seemed to be some guy playing music," though he did not stop. In the nearly forty-five minutes of Bell's performance, 1,097 people passed through the subway entrance. How many stopped to listen? Seven. Though Bell makes about a thousand dollars per minute in concert performances around the world, in the subway station twenty-seven people gave money, most "on the run—for a total of $32 and change." "That leaves 1,070 people," Weingarten writes, "who hurried by, oblivious, many only three feet away, few even turning to look."

The conclusion of Bell's first subway piece, like that of every other thereafter, was met with a thunderous silence. His second piece was Franz Schubert's "Ave Maria," a "breathtaking work of adoration of the Virgin Mary." Weingarten notes that religious interest was uncharacteristic of Schubert, and when asked what led to the sudden piety in his writing this composition, Schubert responded, "I think this is due to the fact that I never forced devotion in myself and never compose hymns or prayers of that kind unless it overcomes me unawares; but then it is usually the right and true devotion." Thus was conceived one of "the most familiar and enduring" pieces of "musical prayer" in history.

And here, in Bell's playing of it in the subway, Weingarten says, "something revealing happens":

> A woman and her preschooler emerge from the escalator. The woman is walking briskly and, therefore, so is the child. "I had a time crunch," recalls Sheron Parker, an IT director for a federal agency. "I had an 8:30 training class, and first I had to rush Evvie off to his teacher, then rush back to work, then to the training

facility in the basement." Evvie is her son, Evan. Evan is three. You can see Evan clearly on the video. He's the cute black kid in the parka who keeps twisting around to look at Joshua Bell, as he is being propelled toward the door. "There was a musician," Parker says, "and my son was intrigued. He wanted to pull over and listen, but I was rushed for time." So Parker does what she has to do. She deftly moves her body between Evan's and Bell's, cutting off her son's line of sight. As they exit the arcade, Evan can still be seen craning to look. When Parker is told what she walked out on, she laughs. "Evan is very smart!" (Weingarten, 2007)

Weingarten goes on to note that there was no ethnic, demographic, or other pattern to distinguish those who stopped to listen to Bell that morning except one: "Every single time a child walked past, he or she tried to stop and watch. And every single time, a parent scooted the kid away." He quotes the poet Billy Collins, who "once laughingly observed that all babies are born with a knowledge of poetry, because the lub-dub of the mother's heart is in iambic meter. Then, Collins said, life slowly starts to choke the poetry out of us. It may be true," Weingarten notes, "with music, too."

On Losing Touch with the Child as Artist

How does life accomplish this? How is it that life, in Collins's words, "slowly starts to choke the poetry" out of the child each of us once was and out of the children now entrusted to our care? How is it that children begin to lose confidence in the artists or aesthetes they are, or once were, lose the creative abandon they once showed when handed some crayons and a blank piece of paper? When do we lose the capacity to recognize and delight in beauty around us? How do we learn to stop hearing what we hear, seeing what we see, knowing what we know?

The actions of Evan Parker's mother in the subway station entrance offer one possible clue as she, in Weingarten's words, "deftly moves her body between Evan's and Bell's, cutting off her son's line of sight. As they exit the arcade, Evan can still be seen craning to look." It is a swift and simple gesture and one familiar, I assume, to most parents, this blocking of a child's line of sight by a parent's body, a physical act rich with metaphoric resonance. A mother uses her body to prevent her son from seeing the beautiful, from hearing what he wants to hear, though he cranes his neck to see and to hear to the bitter end.

Is it through an accumulation of just such unremarkable actions as this that life slowly starts to choke the poetry out of us? To borrow psychoanalytic language, might not so commonplace an action as hers constitute in three-year-olds the psychological headwaters of the defense Freud called *repression*, the mechanism by which one learns to forget without ever truly forgetting the pleasures of one's deepest desires? Or to shift again, this time to language of Christian faith, could not such a singular moment between parent and child signal the beginning of the end of the recognition of the kingdom of God that Jesus finds epitomized within infants and children, the kingdom here another way of expressing the poetry that life slowly chokes out of us? Is this one of the ways that adults, according to Jesus, have come not to know the kingdom they once knew as children?

The Kingdom within and among You

We know that when Jesus speaks of the kingdom of God, he often points to children and, when not specifically to children, to other curiously undersized things or scandalously marginalized persons: "Truly I tell you, unless you change and become like children, you will never enter the kingdom of heaven," we read in Matthew's Gospel (Matt 18:3); or in Luke: "Whoever welcomes this child in my name welcomes me, and whoever welcomes me welcomes the one who sent me; for the least among all of you is the greatest" (Luke 9:47–48). At his most passionate, Jesus prays, "I thank you, Father, Lord of heaven and earth, because you have hidden these things from the wise and the intelligent and have revealed them to infants" (Luke 10:21). Shortly thereafter, "To what should I compare [the kingdom of God]? It is like a mustard seed . . . it is like yeast" (Luke 13:18–21). An infant, a little child, a mustard seed, a smudge of yeast, a lost coin, a pearl of great price— the best things come, for Jesus, in small packages.

So, it is likely no fluke that one of the more puzzling of Jesus' sayings on the kingdom of God—what historical theologian Justo L. González (2010, p. 206) calls "one of the most difficult passages to interpret in the entire Gospel of Luke"—follows sharp on the heels of the account of Jesus' healing of ten lepers, only one of whom, doubly ostracized because a Samaritan, returns to give thanks. The small, the insignificant, the lost and ashamed together constitute the warm-up act for Jesus' remarks on the kingdom in Luke 17:

> Once Jesus was asked by the Pharisees when the kingdom of God
> was coming, and he answered, "The kingdom of God is not com-
> ing with things that can be observed; nor will they say, 'Look, here
> it is!' or 'There it is!' For, in fact, the kingdom of God is among
> you." (Luke 17:20–21)

That one little word *among*, in the phrase "the kingdom of God *is* (present tense) *among* (*entos*) *you* (plural)," has been cause for consternation among interpreters of this passage, principally because it also can and, I submit, probably should be translated as *within*: "the kingdom of God is *among* you"; "the kingdom of God is *within* you." Among or within you? Which is it? *Where* is it, that kingdom?

As New Testament scholar Robert C. Tannehill (1996, p. 259) points out, "the kingdom *within* you" option does not receive wide support from current scholars, to put it mildly, because it emphasizes "an inward, spiritual reality," whereas Jesus, they tend to claim, concerns himself with outward actions and events. In addition, since Jesus here is said to be addressing Pharisees in the plural, he could not possibly attribute to *them*, his opponents, the thinking goes, an inward piety exemplary of the kingdom of God (see also Craddock, 1990, p. 205; González, 2010, p. 206; Fitzmyer, 1986, p. 1161; Ringe, 1995, p. 222; Johnson, 1991, p. 266). Instead, they conclude, Jesus must mean either that he himself embodies the kingdom among them (Green, 1997, p. 630) or that the kingdom is disclosed in relationships among people (González, 2010, p. 207).

Each of these points has merit, and I have no qualms with imagining certainly Jesus or even, though a greater stretch, human communities as bearing us the kingdom. But I must confess that the knee-jerk bias of a number of these interpreters, who presume that sociological dynamics among persons somehow exemplify the kingdom in ways that psychological dynamics within them cannot, stirs me to want to lobby in behalf of the kingdom of God *within* you, *within* me, *within* us.

As John W. Miller (1997) recognizes in *Jesus at Thirty: A Psychological and Historical Portrait*, Jesus' mission is most vividly distinguished from that of his mentor John the Baptist in his ceasing to fast, pray, eat, and even baptize "in the manner taught him by John":

> Since these practices were essentials of John's program of purifi-
> cation for penitents . . . , the fact that Jesus abandoned them . . .
> may be due to a uniquely personal "breakthrough" on his part
> with respect to how a person is made right with God (Luke 18:14).

> It is not something *outside* a man "which by going into him can
> defile him," he began teaching (Mark 7:15) . . . "But the things
> which come out of a man [evil words and thoughts] are what defile
> him" (Mark 7:20). It follows that a person's purification is also not
> accomplished through something external (ritual washings, or
> even outwardly flawless Torah-obedience), but through "cleansing
> those things which are within" (Luke 11:41). (pp. 86–87)

External actions and relationships are not the only things important to
Jesus. Psychological concerns, to put it anachronistically, also matter to
him. Miller makes clear that "without fanfare or ritual, simply and directly,
according to the requirements of each situation," Jesus healed not only
the physical bodies of individuals but also their inner worlds, "sometimes
exorcising (Mark 1:25–26), sometimes healing (Mark 1:29–31), sometimes
forgiving (Mark 2:5), sometimes forgiving *and* healing (Mark 2:10–12).
Often astonishing things happened by means of a few simple words, so that
people marveled at his authority (Mark 1:27, 2:12)" (Miller, 1997, p. 87; see
also Capps, 2008).

Contrast Miller's view to that of Luke Timothy Johnson (1991, p. 266),
among those New Testament scholars wary of psychology, who, while certain that the "whole point" of Jesus' proclamation of the kingdom is "signaled by his healings and those of his apostles," appears to segregate out
bodily healings from those of hearts and minds. Physical healings somehow prove that Jesus' kingdom is "real," Johnson assures us, "not merely a
matter of 'internal awareness.'"

Noted psychiatrist and medical anthropologist Arthur Kleinman
(1980) would likely challenge Johnson on this distinction. He asserts that "a
key axiom in medical anthropology is the dichotomy between two aspects
of sickness: disease and illness. *Disease* refers to a malfunctioning of biological or psychological processes, while the term *illness* refers to the psy-
chosocial experience and meaning of perceived disease" (p. 72). Notice that
Kleinman includes a psychological component in his definitions of both
disease *and* illness, highlighting, as Donald Capps (2008) has pointed out,
that "some organic symptoms are due to psychological factors or causes,"
even as organic factors contribute to psychological distress (p. xvii).

But perhaps Johnson's dismissive "merely," in splitting Jesus' "real"
kingdom from events that are "merely a matter of 'internal awareness,'" can
be excused on grounds that Johnson had no access at the time to the sage
wisdom that novelist J. K. Rowling's (2007) powerful and kindly wizard

Dumbledore offers his protégé Harry Potter in an ethereal eschatological exchange at a deserted King's Cross railroad station in London ("King's Cross" here Rowling's apt moniker, one imagines, for the entrance to the kingdom of God) after both Dumbledore and Harry have died (or in Harry's case only possibly has died). At the end of their dreamlike conversation Harry asks Dumbledore, "Is this real? Or has this been happening inside my head?" Dumbledore responds, "Of course it is happening inside your head, Harry, but why on earth should that mean that it is not real?" (p. 723)

Permeating Worlds

More acerbic among the antipsychologists is Fred B. Craddock (1990, p. 205) in his rant against interpreters who opt for *the kingdom within you* over *the kingdom among you*. To translate *entos humōn* as "within you," he says, is evidence of a "heavily psychologized" culture "whose premiums are on self-realization and the therapeutic values of religion," though I would gladly count myself among those, guilty as charged, who find great worth in both self-realization and the healing power of religion (see Capps, 1993, p. 115). His prose mystifies: "Extreme individualism and the subjective captivity of the gospel are conditions so prevailing in the churches as well as in society that the reader of these comments will undoubtedly already have thoughts on the matter that run far ahead of these sentences" (Craddock, 1990, p. 205). But Craddock fails to note that he would have to include among those touting the therapeutic value of religion every Latin church father who commented on this text.

The early church fathers, rarely charged with being heavily psychologized or with holding the gospel captive to subjectivity, in every instance translated Jesus as saying that "the kingdom of God is within you" (*intra vos est*). Cyril of Alexandria: "[The kingdom] is within you" (Just, 2003, p. 271). For Gregory Nyssen (Plummer, 1956, p. 406), *within you* means the image of God bestowed upon all persons at birth. Or John Cassian: "When the kingdom of God is within you, there is righteousness, peace and joy" (Cassian, *Conference I:13*, in Just, 2003, p. 271).

Equally compelling in support of *the kingdom within you* is Joseph A. Fitzmyer's (1986, p. 1161) claim that if Luke had wanted to say *among you*, he could have done so by choosing a term he uses elsewhere, *en mesō*, where, for example, in Luke 2, the boy Jesus is found in the temple sitting *among* the teachers (Luke 2:46); or when, in Luke 8, Jesus tells in the parable of the sower that some seeds fell *among* the thorns (Luke 8:7); or again, in Luke 10, when Jesus sends out seventy of his followers "like lambs *among* the wolves" (Luke 10:3). In the kingdom saying in Luke 17, however, the gospel writer chooses not the common preposition *en mesō* but the quite rare *entos*, a word used elsewhere in the New Testament only once, in Matthew 23:26, where it designates the *inside* of a cup that Jesus, again speaking to Pharisees, says is more important to keep clean than its outside (Culpepper, 1995, p. 329).

Cups have insides and outsides, and it is important to know the difference between them lest one pour hot coffee on the lap of one's guest. On the other hand, the inside of a cup is very much open or exposed to, even inseparable from, the cup's outside; inside and outside flow seamlessly one into the other. So perhaps the noncanonical Gospel of Thomas comes closest to the heart of the matter in its hearing Jesus say, "But the kingdom is within you and outside of you" (Fitzmyer, 1986, p. 1157)—the kingdom *within*, the kingdom *among*: our inside and outside worlds, quite important to distinguish from one another, are still very much open to and permeated by each other. To borrow once again Dumbledore's wise teaching to Harry Potter, of course the kingdom of God is happening inside our heads, but why on earth should that mean that it is not real?

So if, as Jesus consistently claims, the kingdom of God is near; and if this kingdom is somehow at once really *among* us in a sociological sense and *within* us in a psychological sense; and if in pursuing this kingdom we would do well, as Jesus evocatively asserts, to compel ourselves to think small—of the tiniest of seeds and most vulnerable of persons—then to inquire how life begins to choke the poetry out of us would be to turn our attention not only to those children entrusted to our care *among* us but also to those entrusted to our care *within* us, to that child each of us once was and who remains to this day within.

The mother of three-year-old Evan Parker and a thousand other adults fail to stop for even a moment in that subway station entrance to notice the "right and true devotion" of Joshua Bell's rendering of "Ave Maria." Would we not expect that their failing contributes to at least a modicum, a tiny particle, of self-doubt in little Evan, as the adults around him model for him how to ignore or distrust his senses, teach him to disbelieve the validity of what he alone wants to pause to hear, imply that it's best to dismiss his own intuitions of the beautiful, of even, we might say, the kingdom of God? He learns in this fleeting moment that he should not desire what he desires, should not delight in what delights him.

Linguistic Body Blocking

A body check, like the one Evan's mother used to scoot him from the subway station, functions as a nonverbal cue for the preverbal child to deflect his attention in deference to the desires of the parent. "To be distracted from one's preoccupations as a child (and as an adult) . . . is a subtle and insidious form of humiliation," however much unrecognized as such (Phillips, 1998, p. 135). It invalidates the trajectory of the child's own sense of wonder and discounts the child's own interests and desires. The world, he learns, is not how he experiences or expects it to be. This discrepancy is what we know of as shame, the culprit most responsible, I suggest, for quashing the child's propensity for attunement to what Jesus is calling the kingdom of God.

But even when children's bodies and interests grow beyond the point of deft physical manipulation, parents and others find alternative ways to shame and control them, usually through another, equally imperceptible kind of body blocking—linguistic blocking. The roots of repression in children—of suppressing the poetry or kingdom within them, especially in verbally adept older children—derive from adults' use of language, above all as children learn from them what words they are not supposed to say.

In his memoir *Telling Secrets,* Frederick Buechner (1991), a Presbyterian minister and novelist, tells of how as a boy of ten he came to intuit from his mother that he should never again speak of his father in the aftermath of his father's suicide. As one would expect, the emotional repercussions for Buechner were severe. The deafening household silence about his father's shameful death lingered for decades. But finally, in his fifties, Buechner dared to begin to speak of his father in an autobiography. Then, in his early sixties, a therapist helped him, he says, not just to "remember forgotten parts of my childhood and to recapture some of the feelings connected with them, which I had discovered as a child that I would do well to forget, but also to suggest certain techniques for accomplishing that" (p. 98).

Among these techniques, she asked him to write about his childhood memories of his father by using his nondominant—his left—hand. "My right hand," Buechner writes,

> is my grown-up hand—a writer's hand, a minister's hand—but
> when I wrote with the left hand, I found that what tended to come

out was as artless and basic as the awkward scrawl it came out in. It was as if some of my secrets had at last found a way of communicating with me directly. [My therapist] suggested on one occasion that when I got home I should try writing out a dialogue with my father, using my left hand for both of our parts. (p. 98)

As Buechner followed her instructions, he became convinced in what emerged from his left hand that "in some sense it really was my father I was talking to" (p. 100):

CHILD: Could I have stopped you, Daddy? If I'd told you I loved you? If I told you how I needed you?

FATHER: No nobody could. I was lost so badly. . . .

CHILD: I've been so worried. I've been so scared ever since.

FATHER: Don't be. There is nothing to worry about. That is the secret I never knew, but I know it now. (p. 99)

Though Buechner describes his left-handed father-son dialogue as "artless" and "awkward," the clean minimalism evident even in this brief excerpt suggests, to the contrary, a moving and artful therapeutic work. His nondominant hand somehow retains and embodies his childhood voice, an anatomically localized mnemonics of childhood. Memories encrypted in his childhood self and adult body provide for him a kind of healing aesthetic: "But even if it was not really my father," he concludes, "what it was most really was a better way of saying so long to him than I had ever been able to say it before" (p. 100). Buechner at last was able to say what as a child he was prevented by the shame and shaming of adults from saying. Of course this dialogue is happening inside your head, Freddy, but why on earth should that mean that it is not real?

Disconfirmation Campaigns

In some children's lives, linguistic body checks take a more extreme form, with psychological consequences even more devastating than those experienced by Buechner. In his book *The Forgiving Self*, psychoanalyst Robert Karen (2001, p. 48) recounts a classic study (Cain & Fast, 1972) of psychiatrically disturbed children's responses to a parent's suicide. The study "found that many of the children had been pressured to believe that they had not seen what they had seen, did not know what they knew." The authors of the original study report that

> a boy who watched his father kill himself with a shotgun . . . was told later that night by his mother that his father died of a heart attack; a girl who discovered her father's body hanging in a closet was told he had died in a car accident; and two brothers who had found their mother with her wrists slit were told she had drowned while swimming. (Karen, 2001, p. 48)

The authors found that if the children continued to believe their own senses in these sorts of cases despite the efforts of adults to persuade them to do otherwise, they were ridiculed or told that they were confusing the circumstances of the parent's death with "something they had seen on TV." This kind of verbal deception and shaming led to a radical mistrust of their own experience among the children, manifesting in these cases in dissociation and severe psychiatric disturbance.

But even in crises less extreme than parental suicide and its subtle or blatant denial, language can be used to lead children to mistrust their inner sense of the kingdom. Karen (2001) suggests that a "disconfirmation campaign" against their children's perceptions is often waged to discredit the cruelty or negligence of parents, as in "How dare you talk about your mother like that!" In such cases, other adults rarely step in to challenge the reactive parent's words. Karen asks,

> What child is able to step outside the orbit of these two beloved and idealized figures and say: "This is not about me. My mother is simply a disturbed person. She is too depressed . . . to love me properly"? What child has the intellectual or emotional resources to say: "My mother is nuts, she accuses me of the most ridiculous things and Dad is too deadened or too enthralled by her to help me; I just have to manage the best I can"? Or, "My parents never should have had children; they don't know how to love and enjoy a child; but I'm okay"? (p. 49)

Quite to the contrary, Karen notes, the more abusive the parent, the more likely to be idealized by the child. In instances like these, subtle and less than subtle patterns of speech function to shame children into nullifying their own senses and desires.

Speaking of Repression

In *Freudian Repression: Conversation Creating the Unconscious,* British so-cial psychologist Michael Billig (1999) reconceives what Freud considered to be his most momentous psychological discovery, that of *repression.* Billig maintains that repression derives in each person's life not from innate or self-contained biological processes but from emotionally invested social, especially rhetorical ones (p. 10). Repression, he claims, is a function of language and of speaking. Drawing on Wittgenstein and others to develop what he calls discursive psychology, Billig argues that the peculiar mechan-ics and actual action involved in the phenomenon of repression stem from rules and practices of ordinary conversation.

Children learn to repress as they learn to talk. More specifically, in learning to speak they learn also what *not* to say. Given that some topics are off-limits in polite conversation, children must learn to repress disturbing desires, including, Billig says, "the desire to be rude" (p. 9). The repressed unconscious is not some "pre-existing 'thing'" or an inherent, inborn entity but instead a pattern of willed forgetting that develops over time through social interaction. Repression is constituted, he claims, by conversation (p. 17). It should not surprise us, he points out, that even as talking becomes the principal means by which *healing* occurs in the psychoanalytic "talking cure," so too is talking the source of the *symptoms* that necessitate such a cure.

Billig makes clear that contrary to a popular misconception, Freud never claimed that his greatest innovation was discovering the *unconscious.* Instead, Freud considered his breakthrough to be his discovery of *repres-sion.* In an autobiographical essay written at the age of sixty-eight, Freud (Billig, 1999, pp. 14–15; citing Freud, 1924/1986) reports that the chief discovery of the new science of psychoanalysis was its revealing the process by which human desires are prevented "access to consciousness": "I named this process *repression*; it was a novelty, and nothing like it had ever before been recognized in mental life . . . The theory of repression became the corner-stone of our understanding of the neuroses" (Billig, 1999, p. 15; cit-ing Freud, 1924/1986, p. 213).

Freud sought to parse this distinction between repression and the un-conscious in part because certain aspects of unconscious experience appear to be self-evident and altogether unremarkable. Citing an example from John Searle (1992, pp. 154–55; in Billig, 1999, p. 15), Billig notes that while we may believe that the Eiffel Tower is in France, this belief is not typically conscious to us unless, as in the present sentence, someone makes mention of it. Thus would Freud distinguish between a somewhat commonplace unconscious that he called the *preconscious*, consisting in those latent thoughts and memories not immediately conscious only because at a given moment one is thinking of something else; and the far more mysterious, compelling, and sometimes debilitating *repressed unconscious*, a storehouse of unacceptable thoughts and desires largely irretrievable and unknown even to the one who harbors them.

It is this latter kind of mental content, according to Freud, that has been "repressed" (*Verdrängung*), which is to say "pushed away" or "thrust aside" (Billig, 1999, 15–17). Such thoughts, Freud determined, "*cannot* become conscious*," because "a certain force opposes them" (Billig, 1999, p. 16; citing Freud, 1923b, p. 352). Thus repression involves, in Billig's words, a kind of "self-deceit" or "willed forgetting" of beliefs so repulsive as to be kept, via defensive strategies, from entering consciousness: "If we have secrets from ourselves, then not only must we forget the secrets, but we must also forget that we have forgotten them" (Billig, 1999, p. 13)—repression, then, Freud's term for this latter kind of metaforgetting. Repression is, to borrow British psychoanalyst Adam Phillips's (1994) words, a way "of retaining things by getting rid of them . . . Everything bad is put outside by projection, or into the outside that is inside—the unconscious—by repression. You can, so to speak, forget outside or forget inside" (pp. 22–23). So also, we might extrapolate, you can forget the kingdom among you or forget the kingdom within you.

While a degree of repression is essential for maintaining life together in community, Freud found that in certain individuals to a greater extent but in all persons to a lesser degree the strategies to self-contain the secrets become symptomatic and even more debilitating than would be their actual admission to conscious awareness. Symptoms, Freud said, are reminders of the "return of the repressed." They are, again to quote Adam Phillips (1994), "a person's always unsuccessful attempts at self-cure for memory" and reminders "of our own disowned counterparts," of our categories "of the unacceptable, or unbearable" (pp. 22–24). In these instances, then, and against such defenses Freud labored to assist afflicted persons in their process of remembering by means of the talking cure.

Tearing the Said from the Not-Said

Billig notes, however, that though the idea of repression is pivotal to psychoanalytic thought, Freud remained surprisingly mute about the ways individuals actually *learn* to repress or about the specific mechanisms by which it occurs (Billig, 1999, p. 27). With what Billig calls "characteristic intellectual honesty," Freud himself actually acknowledges his evasiveness on this point. In his *New Introductory Lectures*, Freud, then in his sixties, asks, "What kind of mental impulses are subject to repression? By what forces is it accomplished? And for what motives?" He answers his questions, or rather avoids answering them, by saying that "so far we have only one piece of information on these points," namely, that repression "emanates from the forces of the ego" (Billig, 1999, p. 27; citing Freud, 1933b/1987, p. 339). But Freud's agnosticism concerning the mechanisms of repression does not thwart his zeal for considering its effects. He is, after all, first and foremost a physician, not a metaphysician, whose primary goal is to assist suffering patients.

Billig, for his part, seeks to fill this gap in Freud's theory concerning the mechanics of repression. He attempts to do so not by appealing to an abstract metapsychology of the structure of the mind, as Freud was inclined to do in suggesting that repression emanates from the ego. Rather, Billig focuses on more observable, experience-near behaviors and interactions among persons, particularly, as noted, ordinary rhetorical processes. For him, routine conversation with significant others subtly instructs children in repression, for better (in terms of the importance of their learning rules for polite conversation) and for worse (in terms of the potential for rigidity, compulsion, melancholy, and self-deception that derive from not speaking and eventually no longer consciously knowing their deepest desires and truths).

Routine actions, including routine conversations, occupy an intermediate space, for Billig, between conscious and unconscious thought: "When we act routinely, we might know we are performing the routine but we are unaware of all we do. Our mind might be on other things" (Billig, 1999, p. 37). Billig links routine social conversation to internal thought processes by noting that we often discover what we *think* only by attempting to put words to our thoughts as we *speak*; and even solitary thinking or writing processes involve a kind of internal conversation with ourselves or an imagined partner or audience (Billig, 1999, p. 48).

In writing autobiographically about experiences of severe mental illness, Mark Vonnegut (2010) seems to confirm this latter point in suggesting that "writing is very hard mostly because until you try to write something down, it's easy to fool yourself into believing you understand things. Writing is terrible for vanity and self-delusion. [Writing for me] wasn't therapy as much as trying to tell a story that took me by surprise" (p. 44). As for Vonnegut with writing, so too for Billig with speaking: we learn what we think only by actually saying something, often something surprising even to ourselves.

Language—that used for conversing and that essential to thinking—is always at once expressive and repressive: "We push away disturbing thoughts in much the same way as we avoid troublesome topics in conversation" (Billig, 1999, p. 38). Since "no speaker can be making two utterances at once," it follows that "every utterance . . . is occupying a moment which might have been filled by an infinity of other utterances . . . As Roland Barthes wrote, 'The *said* must be torn from the *not-said*'" (Billig, 1999, p. 52; citing Barthes, 1982, p. 129, italics original).

As they learn to speak, then, young children also begin to formulate the not-said. Billig points out that we subtly construct the not-said in routine conversation through deceptively small words such as "but" or "anyway," which indicate both that we disagree with our conversation partner or wish to change the subject, and that we hope to keep the conversation going. How does one accomplish this without cutting off dialogue? By disagreeing without being disagreeable, almost imperceptibly, using overlooked rhetorical markers such as "Yes, but," whereby the *yes* indicates affirmation of the conversation partner and the *but* signals disagreement with the partner or an impending topic change (Billig, 1999, p. 53). Although changing the subject by way of these small "discontinuity markers" is not identical to repression, Billig notes that an astute "observer might suspect that the movement *away* is dominating the movement *toward*, especially if the speaker continually changes the subject when a particular topic is mentioned" (p. 53; italics original). Thus, repression at its most basic, for Billig, is "a form of changing the subject. It is a way of saying to oneself 'talk, or think, of this, not that'" (p. 54):

> Language, or rather dialogue, provides the means of repression. Because we possess the little words to effect shifts of topic, we can move dialogues, including our inner conversations, from awkward to safer matters. We can say 'but . . .' or 'anyway . . .' to ourselves, just as we can utter those words to fellow conversationalists. (p. 67)

Revisiting Little Hans

To demonstrate how this process of repression develops especially in the lives of young children, Billig (1999, pp. 104ff.) devotes two detailed chapters to a reinterpretation of one of Freud's (1909/1990) most famous case studies, that of "Little Hans," discussed in his essay "The Analysis of a Phobia in a Five-Year-Old Boy." Little Hans was a pseudonym for Herbert Graf, whose mother, prior to her marriage, was one of Freud's patients, and whose father, Max Graf, a music critic who sought to apply psychoanalysis to understanding art, was for a number of years a member of a group of men, later to become the Vienna Psychoanalytic Society, who met in Freud's home each Wednesday evening to discuss psychoanalysis (Billig, 1999, p. 109). With Freud's encouragement, the Grafs decided to raise their son according to principles of psychoanalysis and took particular note of the boy's sexual and oedipal interests and concerns. While Freud derived his theory of the Oedipus complex initially from self-analysis as an adult and then from helping other adult patients retrospectively reconstruct childhood memories, he found in Little Hans what he believed to be prospective evidence for the oedipal plight in real time, so to speak, from the vantage of a young child.

Freud focuses his analysis of Little Hans almost exclusively on the *boy's* tensions (a phobia of horses that keeps the boy from leaving the house) and desires (to sleep in his mother's bed), assuming these to be innate and self-contained. Billig, by contrast, concerns himself with the anxieties of the boy's *parents* and with Freud's surprising lack of interest in their assumptions and inhibitions, especially as revealed in snippets of conversation between parents and child recounted to Freud by the boy's father. As one example, Billig notes that the boy's mother found him, at age three and a half, touching his penis. "'If you do that,' she told him, 'I shall send for Dr A to cut off your widdler [the boy's term for his penis].'" But Freud fails to attribute anything of the boy's ensuing "castration anxiety" to the mother's own anxiety about his masturbation, assuming instead that castration anxiety is inherent in early male psychological development (Billig, 1999, p. 113).

At age four, then, the previously happy Little Hans develops a debilitating fear of horses, which his father and Freud attribute to sexual issues related to his fear of castration at the hand of his father as punishment for the boy's oedipal desires for the mother. But because, Freud surmises, Hans not only fears but also loves his father, the boy "solves" his dilemma by transferring his fear of the father onto horses, "which he associates with his father (having noticed the big 'wi-wi-makers' of these animals)" (Billig, 1999, p. 113). Billig points out that on the very same day, in January of 1908, that the boy first expressed his fear of horses, his mother had asked him, "Do you put your hand to your widdler?" When Hans responded that he indeed did so every evening in bed, she instructed that he was not to do this again (p. 114). Two months later, his father told Hans explicitly one morning: "You know, if you don't put your hand to your widdler any more, this nonsense of yours [the fear of horses] will soon get better" (Billig, 1999, p. 114; citing Freud, 1909/1990, p. 187). Reflecting on this series of events, Billig writes:

> The episode is revealing. To a modern reader, it indicates the obsession of the parents with masturbation. It also shows the parents' belief that Hans's fear of horses was connected with his desire to masturbate—rather than to any induced guilt about masturbating. The desire must be stopped, as Hans is told by his father. In so doing, the father is telling Hans to repress, push aside, the desire. But he doesn't tell Hans how to do this . . . Nor does Freud comment on the matter. (Billig, 1999, p. 114)

What Freud attributes to wholly self-generated and self-contained intrapsychic anxieties within the boy, Billig believes rather to be the outcome of communication patterns about masturbation between Hans and his parents. "Freud," Billig says, "relates Hans's problems, and those of other children, to inner desire, not to outer lesson" (Billig, 1999, p. 117). The parents' "actions—threatening violent punishment against a small child for touching himself—are not described in the language of desire. In this story, it is only the child who has aggressive desires" (p. 117).

The Questioning of Our Questions

Billig likewise considers from Freud's essay a fragment of another conversation between Hans, here nearly four years old, and his mother as she undresses for bed:

Mother: What are you staring like that for?

Hans: I was only looking to see if you'd got a widdler too.

Mother: Of course. Didn't you know that?

Hans: No. I thought you were so big you'd have a widdler like a
horse. (Billig, 1999, p. 125; citing Freud, 1909/1990, p. 173)

Billig notes that while here again Freud's discussion of this conversation
focuses entirely on what is going on within the boy's own mind, there is
nonetheless reason to suggest that Hans's mother is "controlling the direction of the dialogue" (Billig, 1999, p. 128), first with her question about why
he is staring at her, which appears to demand a defensive justification on
the part of the boy ("I was only looking to see if you'd got a widdler too"),
and then with her question about why he is asking about this in the first
place, requiring that he produce a rationale for his behavior ("I thought
you were so big you'd have a widdler like a horse"). The mother's responses,
Billig maintains, not only are deceptive (in that she replies "of course" to the
boy's question about whether she has a penis) but also point to a change of
subject: "She implies that the information is obvious. Having given him the
information, there is no need to stare. If he stares again, he will be account-
able and his previous justification will no longer hold: he will now possess
the information which excused the original staring" (p. 128). Next time, in
other words, Hans would do well to *suppress* and then eventually, we can
assume, *repress* his inclination either to stare or to speak of such matters.

But Billig asks readers to imagine an alternative scenario in which
Hans had instead stared at his mother's hands rather than at her nakedness.
In this case, she might well again have begun by asking him, "What are you
staring at?" Hans might reply, "I was only looking to see if you had a wedding ring." Billig continues:

> We can imagine his mother holding out her hand to show the
> ring. She might even say "Didn't you know this was my wedding
> ring?" But in the case of her widdler, she displays nothing. Hans
> learns that this is not something to be displayed to him. Moreover,
> her questioning of his question is preparing him to realize that it
> is respectable neither to try to glimpse the mother's widdler nor
> even to ask about it. His question has been answered. *More than
> that: the question has been questioned.* (Billig, 1999, p. 128, italics
> added)

Hans thus learns through discreet shaming in conversation—the questioning of his question—not only that some parts of the body are not to be dis-
played physically but that some subjects are not to be broached verbally, a
process whereby the *not-said* in due course gets relegated to the *not-thought*.
Through his mother's linguistic body check, not entirely unlike the physical

body check by Evan Parker's mother in the Washington subway station, Hans comes to know that some urgent interests and desires are fated not to be acknowledged even to oneself. The child starts to forget without ever truly forgetting the poetry of the kingdom within, a connection concisely captured in Norman O. Brown's (1959/1985) classic *Life against Death: The Psychoanalytical Meaning of History*:

> Our repressed desires are not just for delight, but specifically for delight in the fulfillment of the life of our own bodies. Children, at the stage of early infancy which Freud thinks critical, are unable to distinguish between their souls and their bodies; in Freudian terminology, they are their own ideal . . . Freud of course neither advocates nor thinks possible a return to a state of innocence; he is simply saying that childhood remains man's indestructible goal . . . With this qualification, it is true to say that Freud takes with absolute seriousness the proposition of Jesus: "Except ye become as little children, ye can in no wise enter the kingdom of heaven."
> (pp. 31–32)

Avoiding the Imagined Catastrophe of Certain Conversations

An accumulation over time of these microphysical and microlinguistic body checks, then, likely tops the list of ways that adults become, according to Adam Phillips (2010, p. 77), "most resistant to talking about the things that matter most to us." "People organize their lives," Phillips (1994, p. 84) says, "to avoid the imagined catastrophe of certain conversations; and they come to analysis, however fluent they may be, because they are unable to speak."

I once heard the poet David Whyte (2009) convey something similar by likening psychotherapy to writing poetry; in both pursuits, he said, you are "trying to articulate aspects of yourself that you didn't know you knew." Or as Tony Kushner (Green, 2010, p. 99), among the nation's most brilliant playwrights and best known for his epic *Angels in America*, puts it in an interview, "If you have value as an artist it's probably going to be in your capacity to let things inside you get past things that are placed there to keep you from telling the truth. The more you see things as clearly and coldly as you can, the more value you're going to have."

This capacity, second nature among children, is rare among adults, including most artists. Iris Murdoch (1971, 2001) notes in her 1969 essay

"On 'God' and 'Good'" that "Rilke said of Cézanne that he did not paint 'I like it', he painted 'There it is'" (p. 57). "The greatest art," she writes, "is 'impersonal' because it shows us the world, our world, and not another one, with a clarity that startles and delights us simply because we are not used to looking at the real world at all" (p. 63). But this kind of artistic "success," Murdoch declares, "in fact is rare"; few artists achieve a "vision of the real." But when they do achieve it, and when consumers of art allow themselves to be similarly disciplined in seeing "as much reality in the work as the artist has succeeded in putting into it," then, for Murdoch, "the appreciation of beauty in art or nature is not only (for all its difficulties) the easiest available spiritual exercise; it is also a completely adequate entry into (and not just analogy of) the good life, since it *is* the checking of selfishness in the interest of seeing the real" (p. 63, italics original).

In her book *Black Sun: Depression and Melancholia*, psychoanalyst Julia Kristeva (1992), like Murdoch, similarly extends this antirepressive imperative shared by psychotherapy and the arts (i.e., "your capacity to let things inside you get past things that are placed there to keep you from telling the truth") to the realm of religion: "Aesthetic and particularly literary creation *and also religious discourse in its imaginary fictional essence*," she writes, "constitute a very faithful semiological representation of the subject's battle with semiological collapse" (p. 24, italics added). The artist, Kristeva claims, is someone "relentless in his struggle against the symbolic abdication that blankets him" (p. 9). In other words, returning to Adam Phillips (1994, p. 32), "what the analyst does from the outside, the . . . artist"—and, with Kristeva, would we not want to add the theologian, the preacher, the religious visionary, the saint?—does "from the inside: a sustained, forgetful self-listening. Each of them is finding ways of making the previously unacceptable accessible through redescription or redepiction."

The Truth Will Set You Free

Those who with Kristeva would affirm that ministers and theologians should be included, with psychotherapists and artists, among those charged to battle subtle humiliations that fuel semiological collapse, and then to foster forgetful self-listening so as to make the unacceptable more accessible, would also likely be quick to assert that religion typically functions only in fits and starts in this way. Success in religion, as in art, is rare. Religious language, like other forms of language, is a double-edged sword more often co-opted to usurp rather than to encourage the return of the repressed, the poetry of the kingdom within and among us.

Alice Miller (1981/2008)), the Swiss psychoanalyst whose first book, *The Drama of the Gifted Child*, was a million-copy bestseller that rocketed her to international acclaim, continued in each subsequent book to champion children's rights against emotional and physical abuse at the hands of parents and teachers—including spanking and especially, as occurred in her own childhood, the silent treatment (from her mother for days on end, which pressed Alice too into a world of silence) (Miller, 1991, p. 19). In her book *The Truth Will Set You Free*, written decades later at age seventy-eight, Miller (2001) tells of her own search as a child for religious answers to her many questions about the Bible. Why, she wondered, did God forbid Adam and Eve certain kinds of knowledge, when she knew even as a child that knowledge was a good thing? Why, she asked her religious teachers, did the Bible depict "obedience as a virtue, curiosity as a sin, and ignorance of good and evil as an ideal state?"

Calling to mind Billig's claims for the repression that derives from what children are not permitted to say, Miller writes:

> With the best will in the world I could find nothing evil in what Eve did. If God really loved those two he wouldn't want them to be blind, I thought . . . If an ordinary mortal were to show me something desirable and then say I must not desire it, I would find that positively perverse and cruel. But when it came to God, one wasn't even allowed to think such things, much less say them out loud. (p. 7)

Miller would be rebuffed as a child by her religious teachers either "for having the temerity to query God's omniscience and omnipotence" or, on the other hand, for taking the Bible too literally (p. 6). "Children want to be accepted and loved," she writes, "so in the end they do as they're told—which is precisely what I did. But that did not mean that I had lost the need to understand . . . So I was left alone with my reflections" (pp. 6–7).

What she came to realize as an adult, she said, was that the biblical writers, too, were human, specifically men, who themselves no doubt had experienced unpleasant events "at the hands of their fathers" and who in turn created in the likeness of those human fathers "an image of God with sadistic features that did not strike them as such" (p. 7). She concludes:

> There are countless theological explanations for the motives behind God's inscrutable counsels, but in all too many of them I see

a terrorized child trying hard to interpret the mysterious action
of the parents as good and loving, even though the child cannot
fathom them—indeed, has no chance of fathoming them. The motives behind them are unfathomable even for the parents themselves, hidden away as they are in the dark recesses of their own
childhood. (p. 2)

How much of the kingdom that children once knew, Miller can be understood to be asking, has been relegated to their darkest recesses in deference
to an inscrutable proxy for the kingdom insisted on by their parents and
teachers?

Later in the same book Miller reveals, strikingly for me, that her own
early experiences with church authorities should not be taken to mean that
there are no "enlightened witnesses" to the emotional and religious interests
of children: "One shining example," she says, "is Donald Capps, professor of
pastoral theology at Princeton Theological Seminary, who has never been
afraid to draw on the sources of new insights about childhood and come up
with his own exciting discoveries" (p. 92). Referring specifically to Capps's
(1995, pp. 21–36) book *The Child's Song: The Religious Abuse of Children*,
she finds especially in his work on Augustine's "destructive attitude toward
his son," Adeodatus, an alternative, she says, to emotional blindness to the
significance of childhood events that typifies scholarly work in theology.
While she recognizes that Capps's insights may "alarm" some believers,
they ultimately serve to "open their eyes to the circle of violence in their
own hearts and help them free themselves from the tragic fate of their history" (Miller, 2001, pp. 92–93).

The Courage to Feel the Plight of Our Own History

For the adult Miller it was one thing to be able to come to terms intellec-
tually with how her childhood religious teachers, indeed how the biblical
writers and theologians such as Augustine, contributed to a discourse of
silence and shame that conjured a sadistic God who cast doubt on her own
inner experience. It was quite another for her to dispatch with the emotional and spiritual fallout. In June of 2005, several years after the publication of
The Truth Will Set You Free, the famously reclusive Miller, then eighty-two
and living in France, initiated a correspondence with Donald Capps, a rich
exchange that would continue over the following six months.

In one of his letters in reply, Capps mentions in passing of his having sensed from childhood "that my mother loved my older brother more than she loved me, but it was not until I acquired incontrovertible evidence that she had wanted me to be a girl (after all, her first two children were boys) that I understood just how much of a disappointment I was to her. To know this was remarkably liberating!" (D. Capps, personal communication with A. Miller, July 29, 2005). Miller responds to his revelation by saying that in reading his books,

> I have sometimes wanted to ask you: How does it come that you take the liberty to see and the courage to say the 'forbidden things'? How did you manage to write about Augustine, about Jesus and so many others and to stay true to the facts? So it came not to me as a surprise to read in your letter that you are aware of having been a disappointment to your mother just in the first moment of your life. To feel this is very painful and thus most people deny this pain; they try very hard to become what their mother wanted them to be. (A. Miller, personal communication with D. Capps, August 9, 2005)

Miller goes on to confess that she, too, was born a "big disappointment" to her mother.

Alice's mother had been one of eight girls (and two boys) in her own family of origin and therefore had wanted to be able to present to Alice's maternal grandfather a grandson by which "to become eventually valuable." "My birth," Miller tells Capps, "destroyed this hope." She says it took her many decades to understand "what it means to a newborn that its very essence is not wanted, that it has to be something else." But it was this very discovery that led her "to become aware of the importance of childhood experiences for the whole life." "The courage to see," she writes, "may be nothing else than the courage to feel the plight of our own history. Everything else is easier to bear" (A. Miller, personal communication with D. Capps, August 9, 2005).

But a subsequent letter to Capps offers a clue that even as an octogenarian Miller continued to bear scars of the emotional wounds inflicted not only by her mother but by religious teachers in childhood. It likewise demonstrates that she retained the same dogged determination of her childhood self to get her religious questions answered. By this point in their correspondence she appears to have found in Capps a pastoral counselor safe enough to allow for her posing a risky question.

In my reading of this letter, hints of lingering childhood religious wounds are reflected in the fact that Miller at first hesitates and almost apologizes for seeking Capps's reflections on what she worries may be one of those "inappropriate" religious questions that has "reappeared" within her for quite some time: "I wanted to ask you a question that I first suppressed, thinking it was not appropriate to be asked," she writes. Then later, after the asking, she buffers it once again: "I hope you are not shocked by my question." Her evocative question, of a kind most welcome to pastoral theologians, is this:

> We know from the letter to the Hebrews that at least some people (if not all) thought at that time that a son who is not beaten is not loved; he is treated like a bastard. We can perhaps conclude that a son who was not beaten at all was looking for the last "proof" of his father's love. Can it be thus that Jesus' lack of rebellion against the crucifixion has something to do with his belief that a loving father *must* beat and make suffer his son? So his submission to the cruel end might have given him the certitude, the last proof that Abba loved him like a real father. (A. Miller, personal correspondence with D. Capps, November 28, 2005)

More telling for me than either the content of her rich question or the details of Capps's intricate reply is her sense of both hesitation and supplication in the asking. It is as if over those many decades the religiously suppressed child within her, now drawing nearer to death (which would come some five years later at age eighty-seven), has continued to seek and has at last found a priest wielding both the emotional and intellectual acuity to sustain her unorthodox question concerning the kingdom of God. Even at eighty-two, she was invoking the return of the repressed, attempting to ask what as a child she was not allowed to ask, to know what she was not supposed to know, to be interested in what happened to be of interest, to rejoin the *said* to the *not-said*. "The courage to see," she tells him, "may be nothing else than the courage to feel the plight of our own history. Everything else is easier to bear" (A. Miller, personal correspondence with D. Capps, August 9, 2005).

Finding Language For What Matters Most

Iris Murdoch (1971/2001, p. 71), in the same essay "On 'God' and 'Good'" noted earlier, says that to understand any philosopher's work, we should

69

ask what he or she is afraid of. This question, she says, can help sort out whether in a philosophy "one is saying something reasonably public and objective, or whether one is merely erecting a barrier, special to one's own temperament, against one's own personal fears."

So, too, I am convinced, does Murdoch's question—*What is this or that specific philosopher afraid of?*—apply for our efforts to understand any theologian's work, though for theologians I would ask in addition of what they are *ashamed.* This is because of a long-standing Christian claim, at least from the time of Augustine's *Confessions* forward, as Donald Capps (1983, p. 92) puts it, "that one comes to know God through disclosure of one's own shame," a conviction stemming from the excruciatingly shameful death of Jesus as a common criminal, a death whose "injury to self was incalculable":

> Thus to view life from the perspective of the cross, as Christians do, is to embrace our shameful selves, for Jesus' experience on the cross is the paradigmatic shame experience for Christians. For him the cross entailed self-exposure and incongruity, threat to trust and total self-involvement, tragedy and isolation.
>
> To put our shameful selves aside is to dissociate ourselves experientially from the shame of the cross. On the other hand, to embrace our shameful self is to identify with Jesus and thereby experience God as no longer hidden. As Erik Erikson points out in *Young Man Luther*, Luther saw that "the passion is all that man can know of God; his conflicts, duly faced, are all that he can know of himself." (p. 92)

If Capps is right about this, then it seems to me worth asking whether the particular words about God found in any given theology serve more to reveal or instead to repress and conceal the childhood self and shame of the one who wrote them. Does this or that specific theology consist in words that mainly fortify its author's always unsuccessful attempts at self-cure for memory, words that manage to hold at bay disowned counterparts and categories of the unacceptable and unbearable? Is one's theology, however eloquent, a subtle excuse for changing the subject, for avoiding the imagined catastrophe of certain conversations?

So, my question to readers and to myself, pitifully simple, is this: *What is your suffering?* What is mine? What are you afraid of? Of what are you ashamed? Can we talk for a moment about that? Can we talk, too, about what you desire, about what attracts you and draws you in? What music have you been diverted from hearing, what beauty dissuaded from seeing, what questions deterred from asking?

Is what we have forgotten that we have forgotten more likely to be obscured or to be revealed and finally explored in the light of day by those words about God that we think, write, speak, pray, and believe? Do our revelations reveal mostly our hiding?

Can we imagine the vocation of the minister or theologian, as I aspire to imagine my own as a pastoral theologian, to be a courageous, last-ditch effort to unrepress intuitions of the beautiful we once recognized within and among us as children unconcerned with distinguishing body from soul—our calling one of re-calling that little Evan Parker within each of us straining to linger before Schubert's hymn to the mother of God before his own more earthly mother and then her religious surrogates would body-check the kingdom right out of him?

What if we were to write theology with our left hands, our nondominant hands, our child-hands, write it for a season with crayons or finger paints, and allow ourselves to believe in the resulting awkward and minimalist scrawl that it really was our Lord Jesus or heavenly Father we were talking to and about—theology as our anatomically localized mnemonics of childhood? What if theology at its most relevant, sensual, and heroic is finally our bold attempt to desist for once from habits of questioning our questions and instead to articulate aspects of ourselves that we didn't know we knew; theology as our antirepressive imperative to say against all conventions the words we are not allowed to say; theology as our inner artist's striving against all odds—familial, cultural, ecclesial—to let those forgotten but never truly forgotten things inside us get past other things placed there to keep us from telling the truth; theology as our defiant outcry against the suffocating shame of silence and self-abdication? What if to become a minister, a theologian, a Christian even, a saint, means to become again a child before they took the poetry away?

It is not the future of the church that we theologians "should be concerned about, but rather the finding of languages for what matters most to us; for what we suffer from and for, for how and why we take our pleasures" (Phillips, 1995, p. xvi). Of course the kingdom of God is within you, dear friends in Christ, but why on earth should that mean that it is not real?

"The weight of this sad time we must obey, / Speak what we feel, not what we ought to say," pleads Edgar[1] of *King Lear* there at the very end, here

---

1. In some manuscripts, these words are spoken by the Duke of Albany.

at the very end (Shakespeare, 1997/2007, 5.3.320, p. 392). Speak what we feel, not what we ought to say.

4

The Sacredness of Individuality

Introspection for Refuting States
of Total Conviction in Boys and Men

"It is possible that the most ascetic act is not renunciation of the self, but total self-acceptance."

—PAUL EVDOKIMOV (1985, p. 100),
THE SACRAMENT OF LOVE

A State of Total Conviction

"There's always one moment in childhood when the door opens and lets the future in," writes British novelist Graham Greene (1940/1980, p. 12) in *The Power and the Glory*. In my own childhood at least one such door—what my family called the "barn door"—opened to let the future *in* by first letting something forbidden *out*.

One of my earliest memories is of a time when I was likely three or four, old enough to be out of diapers but still confined to a fenced children's wading area of our local swimming pool. I was enthralled with splashing there one day when I noticed my mother and a friend of hers enjoying an extended laugh from their spot on the lawn near the pool. It became clear only after a time that they were laughing at *me*. My mother finally came over to point out that my penis had emerged from the open fly—the barn door—of my swim trunks, and she helped put me back in place.

It was a disorienting moment. There is no question that apart from my mother's laughter I would not have remembered it at all. From an adult's vantage, it is easy to understand how a parent would find this situation amusing (it *is* funny, after all), a boy absorbed in play while oblivious to flashing nearby playmates and women. But of course this incident was seared into my childhood memory not for its warm humor but for its burning humiliation, for what had to have been my initial conscious association of penis and shame.

In the preface to *Religious Mourning: Reversals and Restorations in Psychological Portraits of Religious Leaders*, Nathan Carlin (2014) refers to an essay in which I told of coming to associate with leprosy my severe case of acne as an adolescent. He notes that my professional interests over the years have focused on issues related to sexuality and the body and rightly infers that these concerns are in large measure autobiographical, suggesting "a deep and personal connection for Dykstra between his personal experience and his public scholarship as a pastoral theologian" (p. ix). I agreed with Carlin on first reading those words, while harboring initial doubts about some of what came next:

> Indeed, if as a child [Dykstra] experienced his body and sexuality as theologically impure (*because, in addition to his medical condition, anti-body and anti-sexuality messages were mediated to him via his religious heritage*), as an adult he has more or less come to advocate the reverse upon recognizing and proclaiming "a God who was as concerned with my body as with my soul." (p. ix, italics added; citing Dykstra et al., 2007, pp. 66–67)

Was it really the case, I wondered as I considered Carlin's words, that my religious or even family heritage was a source of my colonization as a boy by antisexual messages, by antibody antibodies? If in my adolescence someone would have inquired (though no one did), I'd have claimed that my ardent physical modesty was *self*-imposed, not inherited or imputed, even as what seemed my immoderate sexual interests had to be *self*-policed. The lofty standards for living in my particular skin, I would have maintained, were ones dreamed up on my own, though in actual experience less often dream than nightmare.

One excruciating evening when I was fourteen, I became convinced because of a persistent sore on my penis that I had contracted one of the sexually transmitted diseases my health class was seeing depicted in graphic films. I had masturbated during sleepovers with a friend my age over his father's stash of *Playboy* magazines but then had stumbled across a Scripture passage in Romans 1 that I understood as condemning such acts. As a conscientious kid who'd earlier had a conversion experience at a Christian summer camp, I read those biblical words with abject terror. The dual threats of venereal disease in this life and eternal damnation in the next pushed me on that particular night beyond my ability to cope.

I forced myself to write a torturous letter to my mother telling of my fear and pleading with her in it not to tell my father. She read the letter at my bedside while I buried my face in the pillow. She then went down to the living room to show it to my father. To his great credit he called our family doctor, who to *his* great credit told him to bring me right over to his home—not, I assume, out of medical concern but because I was otherwise inconsolable. In one of his finest hours, my father drove me in welcome silence through the darkness. Our irenic family doctor—a small-town general practitioner who, I learned only years later, had served as a decorated army psychiatrist in World War II (*Brainerd Dispatch*, 2001)—took me aside in his living room, looked at my penis, inquired as if in passing to whether we were studying STDs in school, and assured me that everything seemed all right. But he added that if it would help, I could stop by the clinic the next day for a blood test, which, given my desperation and despite the additional embarrassment, I actually did (and, of course, with negative test results). The sensitivity showed to me by both my father and our doctor that night partially redeemed its agony.

"To be ashamed of oneself is to be in a state of total conviction," observes British psychoanalyst Adam Phillips (2002, p. 94), a state familiar in my childhood but perilously entangled with my conviction of faith. Still, even decades removed from childhood and adolescence, I needed a moment on first reading Carlin's words linking my religious heritage to antibody messages to concede the possibility that my early self-loathing might have been something not intrinsic within but imposed from without. The door that opened at the wading pool to allow a boy's penis out at the same time let a precarious future in—a mother's laughter the opening salvo against any effortless possessing of desire and faith.

A Fateful Artistic Bravery

Novelist Henry James Jr. (2016), devastated by the death, in 1910, of his brother the psychologist William James, began writing a succession of autobiographical reflections on their entwined lives, largely in tribute to William. With just fifteen months separating them in age, Henry (called Harry by his family) had long idealized his older brother, to whom he felt close in "affection, admiration and sympathy, in whatever touched and moved him" (p. 5). The brothers clung to each other as constant companions in an endless series of unsettling geographic moves throughout childhood and adolescence. Their wealthy, peripatetic father, Henry James Sr., continually uprooted his wife, Mary, and the family, moving William, Harry, and their three younger siblings from the United States to Europe and back again and again, and from school to school, in unceasing search of an unrealized ideal education for his children. The boys had lived in eighteen different houses, in addition to long residences in hotels, by the time William turned sixteen (Richardson, 2006, pp. 19, 22).

In the second of these autobiographies, *Notes of a Son and Brother*, Henry James (2016) recounts an incident in 1860 that likely signifies a moment, for both Henry and William, when a door opened and let the future in. By all reports, the eighteen-year-old William was showing great promise at that point as a young artist, particularly in portraiture (Lewis, 1991, p. 111). Only months earlier, and soon after the family had settled in Bonn, William had beseeched his father to allow him to return to the United States to study art in the studio of William Morris Hunt of Newport, Rhode Island. This request caused his parents considerable consternation because they had moved the family to Europe the previous year specifically to attempt to redirect William's career interests away from art to science (Lewis, 1991, p. 96; Richardson, 2006, p. 11). But Henry also noted that despite their father's vocational ambitions for his sons, Henry Sr. tended, "after a gasp or two," to allow the boys to pursue "whatever we seemed to like." Thus, heeding William's plea, the family returned to Newport in the summer of 1860 in order for him to begin studying art with Hunt (Lewis, 1991, p. 97).

According to James family biographer R. W. B. Lewis (1991), Hunt had only two full-time students in the fall of 1860, William James and John La Farge, himself a gifted young artist (see Figure 1, below) over whom William enthused (p. 109). Seventeen-year-old Henry would tag along with his brother to the studio, where William and La Farge would spend a good portion of the day drawing and painting on the second floor of the house while Henry busied himself with copying plaster casts on the ground floor.

Figure 1. *William James* by John La Farge, c. 1860. Oil on cardboard. National Portrait Gallery, Smithsonian Institution, Washington DC. Gift of William James IV.

In his autobiography, Henry James (2016) tells of one day when he wandered upstairs in the studio to see what the older youths were doing. There, he was stunned to find "the beautiful young manly form of our cousin Gus Barker," an affable and athletic eighteen-year-old redhead visiting in Newport during a Harvard vacation, "perched on a pedestal and divested of every garment" (p. 311) as William and La Farge sketched him. This was Henry's first exposure to a life model, and he recounts that the sight of their cousin standing imperturbably naked on the pedestal had the instant effect of disabusing Henry of any artistic ambitions he had harbored by way of emulating William. This vision of their cousin "forced" him, he said,

> to recognize on the spot that I might niggle for months over plaster casts and not come within miles of any such point of attack. The bravery of my brother's own in especial dazzled me out of every presumption; since nothing less than that meant drawing (they were not using colour) and since our genial kinsman's perfect gymnastic figure meant living truth, I should certainly best testify to the whole mystery by pocketing my pencil. (Henry James, 2016, p. 311; see also Lewis, 1991, pp. 110–111)

In overwrought reaction to what he had witnessed, Henry would never again return to Hunt's studio or aspire to drawing—a boy's "pocketing [his] pencil" in many ways analogous, I suppose, to shutting his barn door "to the whole mystery."

Donald Capps (1997), in a chapter in *Men, Religion, and Melancholia: James, Otto, Jung, and Erikson* on the sources of William James's lifelong melancholia, clarifies what Henry James implies but leaves unspoken in his depiction of events in the studio that day, namely, that William's "bravery" consisted specifically in "the very act of daring to behold and portray the naked body of another young man" (p. 55). This so-called bravery, as noted, had immediate ramifications for Henry, who would turn instead to writing fiction as his chosen art form—even while he would retain and preserve for decades William's life drawing of their cousin Gus, who would die at twenty-one as a Union cavalry captain in the Civil War (see H. James, 2016, pp. 108, 311). But Henry's reaction, or overreaction, to the sight of their naked cousin, Capps speculates, had even more far-reaching consequences for William, not only in relation to his future vocation but also to the precarious state of his mental health.

Despite unwavering passion and success—Henry James (2016, p. 312) credibly likened young William's 1861 portrait in oils of another of their cousins, Katherine Temple, to the work of Édouard Manet—William, too, would mysteriously abandon his own pursuit of art just months after sketching his cousin Gus. At nineteen, he would enroll instead, but with little enthusiasm, in a program of scientific study (Richardson, 2006, p. 41) followed by medical school at Harvard, though he had no intention of ever practicing medicine (Perry, 1948/1976, pp. 72–73). According to biographer Robert D. Richardson (2006), William saw his medical degree "as the end of something, not the beginning"; on receiving it he wrote to a friend, "So there is one epoch of my life closed" (p. 103). He was twenty-seven.

Because of the abrupt nature of William's shift from art to science and medicine, biographers often venture that William's father must have orchestrated it (Perry, 1948/1976, pp. 35, 60). But Lewis (1991) notes that "there is no hard evidence at all to support such a suspicion," especially given Henry's claim that their father regularly discouraged his sons from making *any* final vocational commitments, preferring that they preternaturally keep all options open. Their father wanted his sons less to *do* something, Henry recalls, and more, rather, just to *be* (p. 112; see also Myers, 1986, pp. 19–20).

Capps concurs with Lewis's skepticism over Henry Sr.'s role in William's decision to withdraw from painting, speculating that the boys' mother was likely the more culpable parent. From childhood, Harry was his mother's favored son, "the one who gave her the least trouble" (Richardson, 2006, p. 218; see also Myers, 1986, pp. 23, 39), and she was already encouraging him, at seventeen, in his initial attempts at writing short stories. Capps (1997) speculates that Henry almost certainly would have recounted to his mother what he had witnessed of William and their cousin that day, particularly as a way to justify his own refusal afterwards to return to Hunt's studio. Capps finds it likely that Mary would have held grave reservations about William's chosen art form and, specifically in response to Henry's report, moral trepidations centering on William's "susceptibility to homo-eroticism" (p. 217, n. 10) in the studio. As a result, Capps reasons, it was Mary, hovering in the background, who likely provided impetus for a swift conclusion to William's artistic pursuits:

> As Henry was his mother's confidant, we may guess that he told her the circumstances that led to his decision not to return to the art studio. Perhaps it was this episode that 'inspired' their father to write a friend of his, inquiring as to how he might find a microscope to give his son William as a Christmas gift, a none-too-subtle pressure on William to consider a scientific career instead. (p. 55)

"Daring to behold and portray the naked body of another young man," in other words, may have come to cost young William his dreams but also, as I consider next, to conjure his nightmares.

Despondency with a Religious Bearing

In his chapter exploring the sources of William James's melancholia, Capps (1997) points to Gerald E. Myers's observation that James "suffered from a variety of psychosomatic illnesses throughout his life, including angina, backaches, fatigue, and depression, and that he was willing to try any practical remedy that might alleviate the suffering" (p. 28). But Myers points out that although James held "that his melancholia, like his other conflicts, had psychological causes, he also believed that melancholia 'is more philosophical and less medical than angina. Certain kinds of depression intensify or diminish simply in response to the ideas or beliefs which happen to occupy the mind'" (Capps, 1997, p. 28; citing Myers, 1986, p. 51).

Myers (1986) also notes, "William's first neurotic symptoms, such as inexplicable eye and digestive problems and anxiety," occurred shortly after he abandoned, at nineteen, his career aspirations in art and intensified throughout the entire decade of his twenties. Along with other James biographers, Myers points to "father-son tensions" as "a critical factor in making William chronically depressed" (p. 20; also in Capps, 1997, p. 53). George Cotkin (1994) similarly posits that it was William's father, "through tactics of remonstrance, manipulation, and guilt inducement," who quashed his son's artistic hopes and led him reluctantly "to enter science as a vocation" (p. 45; also in Capps, 1997, p. 54).

Capps (1997) finds no reason to deny that Henry Sr. played a role in William's decision to abandon art (p. 54), but he finds puzzling the almost complete lack of regard among biographers for any part played by William's mother. Where is Mary James, he wonders, in these discussions? For his part, Capps does implicate Mary, specifically, as noted, around her anxiety concerning homoeroticism, and sees the suppression of William's artistic aspirations as an example of what James himself would later refer to as an "abandoning" or even "murder" of the self that occurs in ordinary processes of making life decisions. James (1896/1956) writes:

> Whether a young man enters business or the ministry may depend on a decision which has to be made before a certain day. He takes the place offered in the counting-house, and is *committed*. Little by little, the habits, the knowledges, of the other career, which once lay so near, cease to be reckoned among his possibilities. *At first, he may sometimes doubt whether the self he murdered in that decisive hour might not have been the better of the two;* but with the years

such questions themselves expire, and the old alternative *ego*, once so vivid, fades into something less substantial than a dream. (p. 227; as cited in Capps, 1997, p. 51, italics added by Capps)

This kind of self- or soul-murder is what occurred when William abandoned his genuine promise as an artist, Capps maintains, though he challenges James's claim that irksome internal doubts about such decisions eventually expire. Instead, Capps asserts, these doubts go underground, relegated to the unconscious.

In addition to chronic vocational uncertainty and the numerous psychosomatic symptoms that Myers notes, James would also come to experience severe emotional struggles throughout his twenties. At one point in a letter to a friend, Tom Ward, twenty-six-year-old William writes of having been "on the continual verge of suicide" (Richardson, 2006, p. 83). His struggle culminated in 1870, at age twenty-eight, in what decades later, masking himself as a "French sufferer"[1] in his 1901 Gifford Lectures, subsequently published as *The Varieties of Religious Experience* (James, 1902/1982b, pp. 159–60; Richardson, 2006, pp. 117–20), he would reveal as the "worst kind of melancholy," which "takes the form of panic fear." His despondency as a young man led to "a horrible fear of [his] own existence," alongside a fear of going outside in the dark alone and a general dread of being left alone.

Because he embodies in this period of self-loathing what Phillips (2002, p. 94) refers to as a state of total conviction, it is perhaps unsurprising that James (1902/1982b) confesses that these experiences had for him "a religious bearing," his fear "so invasive and powerful that if I had not clung to scripture texts like 'the eternal God is my refuge,' etc., 'Come unto me, all ye that labor and are heavy-laden,' etc., 'I am the resurrection and the life,' etc. I think I should have grown really insane" (p. 161; Richardson, 2006, p. 118). In a telling paragraph of a memorial tribute to James, his former student John Jay Chapman (1996) intuits this link between James's displaced artistic interests, his melancholia, and his religious predilections:

> There was, in spite of his playfulness, a deep sadness about James. You felt that he had just stepped out of this sadness in order to meet you, and was to go back into it the moment you left him. It may be that sadness inheres in some kinds of profoundly religious

1. See Capps (2015, pp. 76–77, n. 97) for a review of incontrovertible evidence among biographers that James himself was the pseudonymous "French sufferer."

characters—in dedicated persons who have renounced all, and are constantly hoping, thinking, acting, and (in the typical case) praying for humanity . . . It has sometimes crossed my mind that James wanted to be a poet and an artist, and that there lay in him, beneath the ocean of metaphysics, a lost Atlantis of the fine arts . . . For what is there in [metaphysical] studies that can drench and satisfy a tingling mercurial being who loves to live on the surface, as well as in the depths of life? (p. 56)

James's melancholia, however, had not just a religious and artistic bearing, Capps notices, but also a maternal one, for the French sufferer in *Varieties* likewise reveals that "my mother in particular, a very cheerful person, seemed to me a perfect paradox in her unconsciousness of danger, which you may well believe I was very careful not to disturb by revelations of my own state of mind" (James, 1902/1982b, p. 161). In other words, despite the suicidal intensity of his suffering and while living at the time in his parents' house, William entirely "concealed his condition from his mother" (Richardson, 2006, p. 118).

This connection between a man's melancholic temperament, his mother, and his religious attitude undergirds Capps's (1997) conviction that male melancholia "is rooted in a young boy's loss of his mother's unconditional love" (p. 29; see also Capps, 1997, pp. 4, 12–15; Capps, 2001, pp. 150, 157), specifically in the dawning awareness that she is no longer a "perfect" mother fully attuned to her son's interests and needs. Capps draws here on the claim in Freud's (1917/1957) essay "Mourning and Melancholia" that melancholia is a more complex response to loss than is ordinary mourning. In melancholia, rather than being adequately grieved and eventually replaced in the mourner's psychic life, the lost object—in this case, the mother or, more specifically, her unconditional love—instead remains, in Freud's words, in the neighborhood (Capps, 1997, p. 14). The boy has the sense that something has been lost in his mother's shifting affections, yet she herself remains a daily presence in his life. Because it would be too threatening, Capps maintains, for the boy to direct his rage, shame, and sadness over this grave loss to its proper target, the boy's grief, rather than being appropriately mourned, instead is swallowed and directed inward against his own self. As Adam Phillips (2016) puts it, "Originally there were other people we wanted to murder; but this was too dangerous so we murder ourselves through self-reproach" (p. 93).

The emergence of self-reproach in the child thus corresponds, in Freudian terms, with the birth of the superego, which includes the conscience—that "narrow-minded" and "self-critical part of ourselves" whose vocabulary, according to Phillips (2016), is "unusually impoverished" and "relentlessly repetitive":

> There are only ever two or three things we endlessly accuse ourselves of, and they are all too familiar; a stuck record . . . Were we to meet [the superego] socially, as it were, this accusatory character, this internal critic, we would think there was something wrong with him. He would just be boring and cruel. We might think that something terrible had happened to him. That he was living in the aftermath, in the fallout of some catastrophe. And we would be right. (pp. 88–89)

"Conscience," in Phillips's view, thus proves to be "a form of character assassination, the character assassination of everyday life" (p. 93).

Capps (1997, pp. 4, 16) posits that the boy who fears the loss of maternal love seeks out means to assuage the pain, most commonly by attempting to be a conscientious son or good boy, which is the basis for the initiation of his unceasing religious quest for divine recognition, affirmation, and consolation in place of, or as a way to win back, his mother's. "'I will be what you need me to be . . . in exchange for your love and protection,'" the boy unconsciously vows (Phillips, 2015, p. 115). He sacrifices personal desire for the sake of securing favor and faith.

To return, then, to that day in Hunt's art studio when a door opened and let the future in, Capps (1997) maintains that if in the likely event Mary James played a key role in instigating William's shift from art to science in the aftermath of his life sketch of his cousin, this maternal indignity, however indirect, would go a long way toward explaining the severity of William's melancholia throughout the ensuing decade. The lost object in this case—William's pursuit of art as chosen vocation, his "lost Atlantis of the fine arts"—would recapitulate for him, at least in his unconscious mind, the early experience of his first lost object, that of his mother. William's later report of his mother's "cheerful" demeanor and her "unconsciousness of danger" at a time when he was despondent to the point of fearing for his life, all while he was living in her home, leads Capps to charge that Mary's disposition "reflected a refusal to acknowledge that something was desperately wrong with the James family." Mary, it appears, would go to any lengths to disallow insanity in her household (p. 62).

Another Disorienting Discovery

When my mother died some years ago, I was on a summer break from teaching and was the most free among my siblings to prepare her house for sale. I found there in a file cabinet a folder labeled with my name. Taped inside was the decades-old medical report from our local clinic with results of the blood test ordered after that fateful night in my early adolescence. I sat there confounded, reliving its humiliation. Why on earth, I wondered, would my mother have saved this report all those years and left it so accessible? What if one of my siblings, I fretted, or my wife who was helping sort through the house, had found the file first? My mother had to have known this discovery would make me revisit, with little say in the matter, childhood memories flooded with shame. Although I have little doubt that she had compassionate motives in offering this strange missive from the grave, to this day I cannot fathom them. What was she trying to say? What message could she have wanted to send? How would one go about finding out?

The Fallible Utility of Introspection

In "Pragmatism and Introspective Psychology," Gerald E. Myers (1997) laments that William James was "one of the last major introspective psychologists prior to the behaviorist take-over" in scientific psychology (p. 11). Of the method of introspection in his *The Principles of Psychology*, the first and arguably most influential textbook in American psychology, James (1890/1983b) writes: "*Introspective Observation is what we have to rely on first and foremost and always. The word introspection need hardly be defined—it means, of course, the looking into our own minds and reporting what we there discover. Everyone agrees that we there discover states of consciousness*" (p. 185, italics original).

James realizes, however, that consciousness is never a fixed state but rather a rapidly flowing "stream" of subjective feelings, thoughts, moods, and images. In his (James, 1983a, p. 142; see also James, 1884, pp. 1–26) words, "No subjective state, whilst present, is its own object; its object is always something else." Myers (1997) points out that "if a subjective state such as anger is knowable introspectively, it can be present only to a *subsequent* subjective knowing state; that is, what we call introspection is really retrospection" and is therefore "inevitably risky and susceptible to error" (p. 12, italics original). Psychologists and philosophers who comment on introspection today tend to become preoccupied solely with the question of its reliability or fallibility and therefore consider suspect its disclosures (see, e.g., Gilbert, 2006, pp. 43–48, 57–58, 71–74).

But James, though fully aware of its limitations, nonetheless "insisted upon the *fallible utility* of introspection" in psychological investigations (Myers, 1997, p. 12, italics added; see also Myers, 1986, p. 9). Myers (1997) defends James's zeal for the fallible utility of introspection even for purposes of rigorous empirical inquiries:

> When I ask, "Why?" "What does it mean?" "Does it resemble anything in my previous experience?' "Am I really sincere about it?" "Have I been denying (self-deceiving) all along?" "What conception fits this experience best?" and so forth—where what is at issue is a feeling, emotion, mood, attitude, impulse, impression, thought, altered consciousness, and so on—introspection both as observation and retrospection, I submit, is more often than not an essential part of the process of delivering responsible answers to such questions that we put to ourselves. (p. 20)

This may be in part because, according to James (1890/1983b), "*that theory will be most generally believed which, besides offering us objects able to account satisfactorily for our sensible experience, also offers those which are most interesting, those which appeal most urgently to our aesthetic, emotional and active needs*" (p. 940, italics original).

Myers (1997) finds relevance for introspection not just in the kinds of metaphysical questions that tended to concern James but also in contemporary ones surrounding abortion, the death penalty, just wars, and others "that have no bottom lines":

> The only kind of pragmatism that can connect hygienically with this so-called postmodern era, my ruminations tell me, is the Jamesean that is rooted in introspective psychology. We hear much about philosophy as conversation but not nearly enough about it as conversation with oneself. In an era when skepticism, relativism, antifoundationalism, and the death of the author or self cloud the philosophical horizon, the finest irony is that a new sense of *oneself* is needed for finding one's way. Thinking and behaving nowadays requires an ego sufficiently intact to construct, for oneself anyway, a foundation or center of sorts from which and by which intellectual, moral, and aesthetic priorities get developed. Constructing an inner center of convictions that allows a

hierarchy of beliefs and values, thereby escaping nihilism, will be, inevitably, an intensively introspective process. (p. 23)

On a Certain Blindness in William James

Myers (1986) notes elsewhere, however, that James himself, despite his emphasis on the importance of introspection, was not particularly adept at self-analysis and invested no apparent effort to trying to determine the sources of his own melancholia:

> James was skillful in rendering his feelings into words or in record-
> ing his habits and mannerisms, but he was oddly uninterested in
> self-analysis. He could be aware of his tendency to be silent in his
> father's presence, to feel relief when away from his wife, to dread
> being alone, to be assertive toward younger siblings, to dislike ex-
> act disciplines such as formal logic, to escape whenever he became
> a parent, to be endlessly neurotic—yet he was not motivated even
> to speculate about the psychological causes of these phenomena,
> much less to seek those causes out introspectively. (p. 49; see also
> Capps, 1997, p. 28)

James similarly avoids exploring sexual matters in general and his own sexual history or concerns in particular. Paul Woodring (1958) observes that even after James became aware of the work of "his younger contempo-rary, Sigmund Freud," he "gives no attention whatever to the importance of sex when he discusses drives and motives" (p. 11). In James's (1890/1983b) *The Principles of Psychology*, as one significant example of this inattention (though published prior to Freud's early major works), just four of nearly thirteen hundred pages pertain to sexuality. The first of these consists of a single paragraph on sexual function in birds, dogs, frogs, and toads (p. 34), which James curiously summarizes by suggesting, "No one need be told how dependent all human social elevation is upon the prevalence of chastity" (p. 35).

The remaining few pages of *Principles* that reference sexual mat-ters emphasize what James calls an *antisexual instinct* within persons. He describes this instinct as the human impulse for isolation, evidence for which is "the actual repulsiveness to us of the idea of intimate contact with most of the persons we meet, especially those of our own sex." He allows, however, that "very likely most men possess the germinal possibility" for "unnatural vice" that must be held in check by force of habit (pp. 1053–54), though without elaborating on how he learned of this propensity. He then concludes by acknowledging that "these details are a little unpleasant to discuss" (p. 1055) and omits them entirely in the book's condensed version, *Psychology: Briefer Course*, published two years later (James 1892/1992). Thus, in sexual matters James stresses chastity, isolation, repulsion, and homoerotic restraint. John Jay Chapman (Townsend, 1996, p. 65; citing Howe, 1937, p. 199) recalls as a Harvard freshman hearing James lecture on sex to his class, noting that James was "quite young then, and very severe," someone who "left on me a strong impression of stoicism."

James displays inordinate curiosity about all manner of subjects throughout his life (Perry, 1948/1976, pp. 363, 374–75). So his lack of curiosity regarding his own psychological origins, and almost anything having to do with human sexuality in general or his own sexual interests in particular, emerges as a significant blind spot. As Myers (1986) notes, "When it came to understanding the psychological causes for his behavior and that of people close to him, James was like a blind man engaged in target practice" (p. 49). This introspective blindness, however, may help to explain James's claim that one of his least overtly academic lectures, "On a Certain Blindness in Human Beings," best captures the very core of his philosophy and thought—a claim, in turn, that may shed additional light on possible sources of his troubling state of total conviction.

The Sacredness of Individuality

James (1899/1958) confesses that he wishes this lecture—one he delivered, probably to the Episcopal Theological School in Cambridge in October of 1898 (see Richardson, 2006, p. 570, n. 2, on the disputed venue; see also pp. 380–85)—could be somehow "more impressive" because it is for him, he says, "more than the mere piece of sentimentalism which it may seem to some readers" (James, 1899/1958, p. 19). At the publication, in 1899, of the book containing "On a Certain Blindness," James sent a copy to Pauline Goldmark and wrote that he hoped she would read it "because I care very much indeed for the truth it so inadequately tried by dint of innumerable quotations to express, and I like to imagine that you care for it, or will care for it too. What most horrifies me in life is our brutal ignorance of one another" (Richardson, 2006, p. 381). To Elizabeth Glendower Evans he indicated that the essay captured "the perception on which my whole individualistic philosophy is based" (Evans, 1996, p. 66; Richardson, 2006, p. 381).

The "blindness" in the lecture's title refers to James's (1982a, p. 99n; also Richardson 2006, p. 381) conviction "that we are doomed . . . to be absolutely blind and insensible to the inner feelings, and the whole inner significance of lives that are different from our own. Our opinion of the worth of such lives is absolutely wide of the mark, and unfit to be counted at all." In describing the essay in the book's preface, James (1899/1958) writes:

> It connects itself with a definite view of the world and of our moral relations to the same . . . , I mean the pluralistic or individualistic philosophy. According to that philosophy, the truth is too great for any one actual mind, though that mind be dubbed 'the Absolute,' to know the whole of it . . . There is no point of view absolutely public and universal. Private and incommunicable perceptions always remain over, and the worst of it is that those who look for them from the outside never know *where*. The practical consequence of such a philosophy is the well-known democratic respect for *the sacredness of individuality*—is, at any rate, *the outward tolerance of whatever is not itself intolerant*. (p. 19, italics added)

There are things we simply cannot know, from the outside, of the interior purposes and passions of others, and this obliviousness, James (1899/1958) concludes, "forbids us in pronouncing on the meaninglessness of forms of existence other than our own" (p. 169). The perception most sacred to him, he is suggesting, is the necessity of respecting individual difference by means of tolerating whatever is not intolerant.

Abundant biographical testimony underscores how fully James lives out this generosity of spirit in countless relations with others (see, e.g., Simon, 1996). More difficult for him, it strikes me, is affording himself such tolerance on his own behalf. "On a Certain Blindness" likely attains pronounced significance for him not only for its overt altruism in calling for modesty and tolerance when considering others' inner purposes but also because it covertly expresses James's personal yearnings to be tolerated by intimate others and perhaps especially to more fully tolerate himself. Persistent struggles with melancholia throughout his adult life point to a recurrent state of total conviction within him cruelly intolerant of his own tolerant self. The impoverished and repetitive vocabulary of an internalized accuser promulgates in him the character assassination of everyday life. His essay becomes then an unconscious protest against others', even his own, "brutal ignorance" of his hidden interior life but therefore also a plea for greater acceptance, including self-acceptance, of his singular desires as an individual.

To Miss the Joy Is to Miss All

James (1899/1958) begins "On a Certain Blindness" with a revealing personal narrative in which he describes at some length a journey he once took through the mountains of North Carolina. There, in the mountain "coves," James finds what he experiences as unmitigated squalor, in which settlers had cut or killed countless forest trees, "left their charred stumps standing," and in the clearings had built log cabins surrounded by a "tall zigzag rail fence . . . to keep the pigs and cattle out." When James inquires of the mountaineer who is driving him "What sort of people are they who have to make these new clearings?" he is taken aback by the driver's response: "All of us. Why, we ain't happy here, unless we are getting one of these coves under cultivation" (p. 151). James is humbled by this revelation and reproaches himself for his own blindness "to the peculiar ideality of their conditions," even as he recognizes how strange the mountain settlers would find his own "indoor academic ways of life at Cambridge" (p. 152).

But James devotes even more attention in the lecture—a remarkable three-and-a-half of twenty total pages—to direct quotation from a particular chapter, "The Lantern Bearers," of the American travel memoir of Scottish novelist and poet Robert Louis Stevenson (1892, pp. 206–28). There Stevenson recalls, perhaps by means of introspection, the thrill he experienced in his youth in meeting up in the dark nights of September with four or five of his male friends, who would each secretly steal away from their homes while bearing hidden under their coats a lighted tin bull's-eye lantern (see Figure 2). The usefulness of the lanterns, "carried at their belts," Stevenson reports, "was naught, the pleasure of them merely fanciful, and yet a boy with a bull's-eye under his top-coat asked for nothing more . . . When two of these asses met," he writes, "there would be an anxious 'Have you got your lantern?' and a gratified 'Yes!'" (James 1899/1958, p. 152; citing Stevenson, 1892, p. 214).

**Figure 2. Nineteenth-century bull's-eye lantern.
National Railway Museum/SSPL, London.**

The boys would then proceed to find a docked boat in which to gather.
Stevenson continues:

> Then the coats would be unbuttoned, and the bull's-eye discov-
> ered; and in the chequering glimmer, under the huge, windy hall
> of the night, and cheered by a rich steam of toasting tinware, these
> fortunate young gentlemen would crouch together in the cold
> sand of the links or on the scaly bilges of the fishing-boat, and
> delight them with inappropriate talk . . . The essence of this bliss
> was to walk by yourself in the black of night, the slide shut, the
> top-coat buttoned, not a ray escaping, whether to conduct your
> footsteps or to make your glory public . . . ; and all the while, deep
> down in the privacy of your fool's heart, to know you had a bull's-
> eye at your belt, and to exult and sing over the knowledge. (James,
> 1899/1958, p. 153; citing Stevenson, 1892, pp. 215–16)

Stevenson uses these boyhood recollections of clandestine bull's-eye as-
semblies to express, as does James in his nearly breathless appropriation,
how hard it is to ascertain the source or "ground of a man's joy." Sometimes
it comes in the form of an external object or activity, such as in a boy's
secret lantern or in gathering with trusted friends solely for the purpose

of "inappropriate talk." At other times, Stevenson suggests, this joy "may reside in the mysterious inwards of psychology." We cannot always discern this source in another, but "to miss the joy is to miss all" (James, 1899/1958, p. 155; citing Stevenson, 1892, p. 224).

I find inspiration in the lesson drawn by both Stevenson and James around the difficulty and importance of searching out the often-secret source of another's joy. This is the basis for learning to tolerate "whatever is not itself intolerant." Of more immediate interest to me here, however, is the obvious passion James displays in his almost boundless recital of this narrative: "These paragraphs are the best thing I know in all Stevenson. 'To miss the joy is to miss all,'" James (1899/1958, p. 155) ejaculates.

But then he proceeds to miss the joy, specifically the contours of his own joy. He stops short of investigating possible personal sources of his profound identification with Stevenson's narrative. His estimable concern for missing another's joy circumvents any introspective exploration. James's "certain blindness" strikes me in this instance less as a failure to appreciate the "inner feelings, and the whole inner significance" of others' lives and more as a neglect of the inner feelings and significance of his own.

Unspoken Nostalgia for Homoerotic Innocence

What is it about these lantern boys that so fully captivates James? One could speculate that, on a surface level, they call to mind the satisfaction he found as a boy in mild forms of rebellion with childhood peers. In his *Principles*, published two years before Stevenson's memoir, James (1890/1983b) invokes forbidden male bonding to describe how individuals reveal different aspects of self in distinct social settings: "Many a youth who is demure enough before his parents and teachers, swears and swaggers like a pirate among his 'tough' young friends" (p. 282; also in James, 1892/1992, p. 177). He neglects to mention, however, that he himself was one such youthful pirate. In the first of his memoirs after William's death, Henry James (1913/2016) recalls a time in their boyhood when he asked to accompany William and his friends on an excursion. William, however, rebuffed him, saying, "*I* play with boys who curse and swear!" (p. 158). Like the lantern-bearers, James appears to relish clandestine times for "inappropriate talk" with male friends—and not just in childhood. Displaying "a peculiar genius for friendship" (Perry, 1948/1976, p. xix; see also pp. 45, 95, 165, 231–33, 377–78), he draws stability and sustenance throughout his life from intentional, often intimate, contact with other men, including students and colleagues.

In 1876, for example, James, then thirty-four and not yet married, purchased an isolated cabin in the Adirondacks with longtime friends James Jackson Putnam, his brother Charles Putnam, and Henry Bowditch, to which the men would retreat each year for several weeks at a time. George Prochnik (2006), James Putnam's great-grandson, offers the tender biographical detail that James and his friends would bathe there together in the brook each morning and, after a vigorous hike in the mountains, bathe again together in the afternoon (pp. 30, 38). As another indication, James's son Henry James III (1996) tells of how year after year as a Harvard professor his father would assign the family's dinner hour as his regular consultation time with students: "Sometimes he left the table to deal with the caller in private; sometimes a student, who had pretty certainly eaten already and was visibly abashed at finding himself walking in on a second dinner, would be brought into the dining-room and made to talk about other things than his business" (p. 119). W. E. B. Du Bois (1940), a distinguished former student, recalls that he had been "repeatedly a guest in the house of William James" and refers to James as his "friend and guide to clear thinking" (pp. 33, 38; see also Richardson, 2006, p. 316). Josiah Royce (1996), James's faculty colleague in the philosophy department and next-door neighbor, confided to esteemed guests at a dinner party in James's honor, "He was good to me, and I love him" (p. 41; see also Townsend, 1996, p. 188). James Jackson Putnam (1996) observes, "James made no enemies, but usually drew closer and closer, as time went on, the ties of early friendships" (p. 25).

The enduring intimacy of these recurring connections with other men, both young and old, suggests that something beneath the surface of consciousness and beyond the pleasures of piratical swagger may be drawing James to Stevenson's lantern-bearers. His sacred resonance with this text intimates deeper undercurrents at play. Noteworthy in this regard given James's keen psychological mind, though perhaps not surprising in light of his sexual aphasia, is that the homoerotic imagery of Stevenson's boyhood memories appears to escape James's notice (as it likely does Stevenson's own): a forbidden lantern is hidden dangling at a boy's belt through the darkness of night, not a single ray of its light escaping his topcoat, the boy uncertain whether to make his glory public; he meets up with male peers and secretively signals, "I'll show you mine if you'll show me yours";

then these fortunate gentlemen, unbuttoning to expose their lanterns and cheered by a rich steam of toasting tinware under the huge, windy hall of the night, crouch together and delight in inappropriate talk.

The suggestive nature of these images—need I add that bull's-eye lanterns measured seven inches?—recalls to mind something of the absorption of the young artist William James at his easel in Newport that day when the door opens and lets the future in. There, he engages in the intimate, arguably sensual, act of sketching his cousin unclothed. What Henry James perceives as William's "bravery" in, to borrow Capps's words, "daring to behold and portray the naked body of another young man," we might also recognize as William's genuine ease and comfort in the physical, even unconsciously erotic, presence of boys and men. Equally impressive is how at home in his skin is their cousin Gus Barker as life model. There was once a time in these boys' lives, in other words, when "the idea of intimate contact with most of the persons we meet, especially those of our own sex," was not at all as "repulsive" to them as, by the time of *Principles*, James claims it had become. There was once a time when somehow he came to understand that "most men possess the germinal possibility" of sexual longing for other men.

James's bliss over the lantern boys hints of unarticulated nostalgia for an ambiguous eroticism preceding his mother's anxious interventions; for a season prior to the onslaught of the internalized character assassinations of everyday life; for a time before the emergence of that state of total conviction of shame or self-reproach and the onset of religious melancholia. The allure for James of Stevenson's imagery signals an unconscious plea for tolerance of a boy's homoerotic desire that is not itself intolerant. This is the way of boys with their friends, the lantern-bearers summon James to say. This is the forbidden source of a man's joy. This is also likely the hidden menace for James in introspection.[2]

2. Though James was guarded concerning his sexual interests and history, James Jackson Putnam, who at nineteen befriended James as a fellow medical student at Harvard, was in later life more forthcoming. In 1911, Putnam (in Hale, 1971), then sixty-four, reveals in a letter to Sigmund Freud not only that he "dreaded" sexual relations with his wife, which by that point had become "rather infrequent," but also that "affection, readiness to be caressed, narcissism, 'protest,' autoeroticism, homosexuality, heterosexuality—all played large parts in my early life, as also a sense of inferiority ('too small sexual organs,' etc.) and desire for recognition as an escape from inferiority" (pp. 125–29). He confides that a search for influential friends has been one strategy for attempting to overcome this sense of inferiority: "I think I have also tried, as I imagine many others have, to compensate for assumed internal lacks, by external aids—things that I could

Chosen

At age eleven, I experienced, as noted earlier, an emotional confirmation of the faith in which I had been raised. I was attending a Christian summer camp for the first time. The camp was located several hours from my home. Dead last to arrive among the dozen boys in my cabin, I took the only bed available, a bottom bunk. I was anxious. I did not know any of the other boys. I had wanted a top bunk.

That first evening at lights-out, as our counselor prepared to read aloud the opening chapter of what would be an ongoing nightly bedtime story, the alpha-male camper, son of the camp director, pointed to me from his top bunk across the room and said I could join him there for the story. Everyone heard him say this. I could not believe I had been chosen. I could not believe he was allowed to choose. I could not believe that our counselors would let me listen to the story from someone else's bunk. But then, after a moment's hesitation, I believed. I scrambled up to his bed, instantly increasing my social capital among the cabin boys but also, more important, finding in this new friendship an unaccustomed surge of self-confidence that would propel me through the rest of that week. He and I became inseparable in the ensuing days and found ourselves together on his bunk for the story each night. The counseling staff designated us "Cutest Couple" in the final edition of the camp's daily newspaper.

Memories of that camp have occasioned in me a sense of joy long ascribed to feeling embraced there by Jesus, a religious awakening with outsized implications for my life. This aspect of what occurred continues to remain meaningful to me. But reflecting on James's delight in Stevenson's lantern boys or in the pirates with whom as a child he could swear and swagger; reflecting also on James's comfort as a youth in the life sketch of his cousin or as an adult in bathing with friends in the mountain brook; and then coupling these reflections with introspection, which is actually retrospection, around my own early associations of sexual pleasure and shame, I am led to a more complex and perilous truth. This truth is that an eleven-year-old boy's newly energized faith in God serves in part as a cover

---

buy, influential friends, etc." One could plausibly extrapolate from these remarks that Putnam's youthful and enduring friendship with James, as also much later his budding friendship with Freud, though in each case chaste, may have channeled for him erotic undercurrents. For a compelling discussion of same-sex male friendship, including that shared by Putnam and Freud, as homoerotic sublimation, see Carlin and Capps (2015, pp. 20–27, 183). See also Dykstra, Cole Jr., & Capps (2012, pp. 43–69).

for, but also, more benevolently put, as a mirror reflection of, a chaste but charged friendship with another boy. Conscious and respectable religious claims conspire to fuse with unconscious and forbidden erotic bonds. The faith and the friendship become from this perspective indistinguishable, one and the same (see Dykstra et al., 2012, pp. 80–84). To miss this joy, one that not only William James but all boys and men are duty-bound to miss, is to miss all.

One final memo from summer camp: I forgot at some point that week what my mother looked like. I am not making this up. I could not remember her face. For days I worried that I would not be able to pick her out among the crowd at the end of the week. If at camp Jesus had come to stand in for prohibited love, he did so in part by eclipsing my mother's gaze.

It was this gaze I felt burning into me while standing exposed in the wading pool at age four. It was her gaze I sought in vain to avoid by burying my face in the pillow at age fourteen, a scrutiny that would lead me instantaneously, beginning that very night and for years thereafter, to shutter my lantern, to pocket my pencil, to shut my barn door, to excise erotic joy on behalf of spiritual zeal. Decades later, this sense that she was watching still, even from the grave, was for me the most unsettling aspect of finding the medical report in the file marked with my name.

But from another vantage it was no longer her gaze, nor that of family, peers, culture, or even of Jesus, at all. The gaze instead was my own, in some sense now all mine, a fully internalized accusatory character living, in Phillips's (2015, p. 89) words, "in the fallout of some catastrophe." The gaze had come to entail self-murder through self-reproach. I had become a sharpshooter in the interior "character assassination of everyday life" (p. 93). Like James as a young man, I had achieved a sanctified but unsanctionable state of total conviction.

Self-Acceptance as Ascetic Act

No wonder the importance to James (1899/1958) of "On a Certain Blindness in Human Beings" and his deep affinity "for the truth it so inadequately tried . . . to express." If other individuals or communities are "harmlessly interested and happy" in ways not our own, he concludes in his lecture, the appropriate response is "to tolerate, respect, and indulge" them: "Hands off," he implores, for "neither the whole of truth nor the whole of good is revealed to any single observer" (p. 169), including, we might add, the whole of the truth and goodness of James's inner life. *Hands off*, he is saying, perhaps to his mother, possibly to God, more likely to himself. *Tolerate others, to be sure, but tolerate me as well, my artistry, my eroticism. And tolerate yourself. The sources of our joy are scarcely known but sacred.*

Would James ever garner such tolerance on his own behalf? His struggle with melancholia, though seldom to the degree experienced in his twenties, was a lifelong one. There would be no miracle cure. In the summer of 1900, James, at fifty-eight, wrote to his wife from the therapeutic spas of Bad-Nauheim, Germany, saying that he had "*no strength at all*" and that his efforts "to summon up a 'will to believe . . . is a no go. The Will to Believe won't work'" (Lewis, 1991, p. 511; and Capps, 1997, p. 49; James's italics). In "On a Certain Blindness" we find James indulging with a generous measure of grace the peculiar means by which others find joy in their lives. He seems no longer inclined or able, however, to allocate a portion of this grace for himself.

In *The Sacrament of Love*, Paul Evdokimov (1985), a Russian Orthodox layperson living in Paris, writes, "It is possible that the most ascetic act is not renunciation of the self, but total self-acceptance" (p. 100). Its counterintuitive resonance somehow makes this claim sound exactly right. This sort of Christian asceticism seems pretty enticing to me, as I can imagine it might to William James and to other boys and men—total self-acceptance as a refreshing alternative to total conviction. But my question is, Is it possible to totally accept one's desire if one has a mother or a faith? Is it possible to totally accept one's penis without becoming a dick?

Perhaps it is enough, following the lead of Stevenson's lantern boys, to find yourself content, "deep down in the privacy of your fool's heart, to know you [have] a bull's-eye at your belt, and to exult and sing over the knowledge" (James, 1899/1958, p. 153; citing Stevenson, 1892, p. 216).

5

Finding Language for What Matters Most

*Hosting Conversations about Sexuality
in Pastoral Counseling*

*Now when Jesus returned, the crowd welcomed him, for they
were all waiting for him. Just then there came a man named
Jairus, a leader of the synagogue. He fell at Jesus' feet and begged
him to come to his house, for he had an only daughter, about
twelve years old, who was dying.*

*As he went, the crowds pressed in on him. Now there was
a woman who had been suffering from hemorrhages for twelve
years; and though she had spent all she had on physicians, no one
could cure her. She came up behind him and touched the fringe
of his clothes, and immediately her hemorrhage stopped. Then
Jesus asked, 'Who touched me?' When all denied it, Peter said,
'Master, the crowds surround you and press in on you.' But Jesus
said, 'Someone touched me; for I noticed that power had gone
out from me.' When the woman saw that she could not remain
hidden, she came trembling; and falling down before him, she
declared in the presence of all the people why she had touched
him, and how she had been immediately healed. He said to her,
"Daughter, your faith has made you well; go in peace."*

*While he was still speaking, someone came from the
leader's house to say, "Your daughter is dead; do not trouble the
teacher any longer." When Jesus heard this, he replied, "Do not*

fear. Only believe, and she will be saved." When he came to the house, he did not allow anyone to enter with him, except Peter, John, and James, and the child's father and mother. They were all weeping and wailing for her; but he said, "Do not weep; for she is not dead but sleeping." And they laughed at him, knowing that she was dead. But he took her by the hand and called out, "Child, get up!" Her spirit returned, and she got up at once. Then he directed them to give her something to eat. Her parents were astounded; but he ordered them to tell no one what had happened.

—LUKE 8:40–56

Is there something foreordained about the link between sexuality and loneliness? Is this merely the plight of the seminary students with whom I talk (a plight that is not unfamiliar to their teacher)? Whether a culture's sexual ethos is restrictive and repressed, as is often presumed about Freud's, or enlightened and libertarian, as some consider our own, the intimacies that bind us together come replete with loneliness and shame.

Inhibition and Exhibition

I read some years ago an article in the *New York Times* titled "Students Still Sweat, They Just Don't Shower." Dirk Johnson (1996) describes how, at some point in the 1990s, adolescents and young adults stopped taking showers together after gym classes or athletic events, even when mud-covered after football games, an antipathy that puzzles coaches of a previous generation: "'These guys don't want to undress in front of each other,' said John Wren, a [high school] teacher . . . in suburban Chicago, who can scarcely conceal his contempt for the new sensibilities. 'I just don't get it. When I started in '74, nobody even thought about things like this.'" The *Times* journalist points out that "modesty among young people today seems, in some ways, out of step in a culture that sells and celebrates the uncovered body in advertisements, on television and in movies. But some health and physical education experts contend that many students withdraw precisely because of the overload of erotic images—so many perfectly toned bodies cannot help but leave ordinary mortals feeling a bit inadequate." In addition, the high level of awareness and even acceptance of homosexuality in this demographic of American young people paradoxically may add to their increased sense of personal distress in the locker room: "'You never know who's looking at you,' said Vicki Johnson, an eighteen-year-old from Algonquin, Illinois." Or as "Andre Hennig, an eighteen-year-old senior at McHenry High School in the northwest suburbs of Chicago," puts it, "'Standing around together naked? Oh no, man—people would feel really uncomfortable about that.'"

I was chatting with a Princeton sociologist of my own generation about his research plans as we stood in the vast men's locker room of the university's ancient gym. He was looking to find a way, he said, for researchers to observe people in their own homes on a matter of interest to him but was not sure how to attain this level of access to their lives. I told him I had read in the newspaper that some companies that specialize in bathroom shower-heads and shampoo wanted to observe how consumers were actually using their products in their daily routines, so the market researchers proposed filming people "taking real showers in their own homes." The investigators initially worried about how they would be able to find subjects willing to participate: "'We thought it would be hard to recruit people,' said Daniel C. Buchner, [one such company's] vice president for innovation and design, 'but that was the easy part'" (Taylor, 2006; see also Horovitz, 2007). My sociologist friend was amazed to hear that volunteers expressed no qualms about being filmed while showering in their own homes. In this era of reality television, I told him, I was not very surprised.

At the very moment he and I were talking, I could see over his shoulder a university student who had just returned from swimming. The student was going through the contortions of getting out of his swimming suit and back into his street clothes without having to expose himself (and, needless to say, without having first showered). He wrapped a towel over his swimsuit, peeled off the wet suit under the towel, and put on his underwear with the towel still protecting him—a common ritual today among young people.

But despite their locker room reserve, many young men his age—perhaps even the very student I observed—have few inhibitions about displaying themselves online. In their book *A Billion Wicked Thoughts: What the Internet Tells Us about Sexual Relationships*, neuroscientists Ogi Ogas and Sai Gaddam (2012, pp. 40–42) note that in eye-tracking studies, men looking at various images consistently first direct their gaze to the male crotch. They also point out that if "historically, male exhibitionism has been considered a mental disorder," then the Internet today "suggests we are a planet of mentally deranged men." On the website Chat Roulette, for example, viewers see whatever other users choose to put in front of their webcams. A recent study showed that of nearly thirteen hundred consecutive Chat Roulette sessions, fully one-fourth were aimed at a penis. On another website, Fantasti.cc, "23 percent of the male users use an image of their penis as their avatar, while another 13 percent used a penis from a porn clip" (p. 42). "On Reddit's heterosexual Gone Wild forum, where users are free to post NC-17 pictures of themselves," Ogas (2011) notes, "35 percent of images self-posted by men consist of penises," despite the fact that by an overwhelming statistical margin it is men, not women, who show interest in seeing men's genitals: "Men's desire to show their penis is only matched by men's equally natural urge to look at *other* men's penises" (Ogas, 2011, italics original). An exaggerated modesty among young men in the locker room, in other words, does not translate into a lack of interest in seeing other men's packages or in displaying their own.

So I was struck in that conversation with the sociologist by the odd disconnect between what we were discussing, that is, the nonchalance of consumers willing to be filmed unclothed in their own showers, and what I was observing right behind him, namely, the obvious discomfort of an athletic young man with undressing in a men's locker room. The modesty of the young man unwilling to be seen in the locker room concerned me at least as much as did the immodesty of those willing to be filmed in their homes. Intriguing as well is the disparity between young men's reluctance to be seen when in the company of actual men and their hunger to see and be seen in the presence of virtual millions. But most important to me in all this is that the sexual permissiveness or freedom we often presume among young people was juxtaposed in that conversation with evidence of a new expression of their sexual anxiety. The more things change, the more they stay the same.

It matters less whether the sexual conventions of the crowd or culture are restrictive or are libertarian than that certain vulnerable individuals predictably fall prey to them in one or another symptomatic way. Authentic personal conversations about sex and sexuality remain as rare in our era, saturated with sexualized images and messages, as they are in times and places where sex remains secreted away from public view. We continue to find ourselves "most resistant to talking about the things that matter most to us," notes British psychoanalyst Adam Phillips (2010, p. 77). "People organize their lives," Phillips (1994) asserts, "to avoid the imagined catastrophe of certain conversations; and they come to analysis, however fluent they may be, because they are unable to speak" (p. 84). Whatever a given society's sexual conventions, it appears that sexuality and vulnerability, intimacy and isolation, inhibition and exhibition, continue to surface as fated companions. Sexuality and loneliness—perfect together. It is at this unsettling interface where the gifts and resources of ministers who give counsel, though they too suffer these inner ambiguities, come into play.

Foremost among my claims in the present chapter is that *a given society's conventions concerning its range of acceptable sexual interests and practices inexorably take their toll among its more vulnerable citizens.* But as important, as I noted in the Introduction (pp. 4–5), *when our parishioners, students, or counselees summon up courage to confide in us as counselors about the idiosyncratic ways these societal tolls manifest as symptoms in their personal lives, they should feel less lonely rather than lonelier for having done so,* even right from the start. Pastoral counseling, it strikes me, should help people feel better. Counselees feeling better, less lonely, is one clue that the counseling process is on the right path.

The Decisive Therapeutic Event in the Gospels

Nowhere are these claims more evident than in two entangled biblical healing accounts in Luke 8, one of which Erik H. Erikson (1974) described as "the decisive therapeutic event in the Gospels" (p. 48). The approaches of Jesus with a woman who has suffered a hemorrhage for twelve years and in healing the twelve-year-old daughter of a synagogue leader named Jairus dramatize his favoring individuals at the expense of the crowds, especially in these cases individuals whose lives have been severely compromised by social conventions signified by those very crowds.

The crowds reflect nothing exemplary in these narratives. "The growth of the crowds gathered to hear Jesus," writes Joel B. Green (1997), "has not been accompanied by maturation in the general perception of Jesus; indeed, the crowds seem actually to have served as a potential impediment to the communication of good news in these two episodes" (p. 351). "Against this background," Green asserts, the woman "is revealed as a person of faith that survives the test," and similarly, "Jairus and his wife are able to put aside their fear and to embrace faith in Jesus' capacity to bring restoration" (p. 344). In his comments on Luke's Gospel, Justo L. González (2010) points out that Jesus' calling is one "among crowds; but it is also a mission of personal touch" (p. 110). Or as Elizabeth Struthers Malbon (1983) puts it, "The crowd crowds Jesus" (p. 32) and ultimately abandons him. The crowd never quite fathoms Jesus here, though a long-suffering woman does; it ridicules his claims, but a desperate father of a daughter perceived to be dying does not. As important, Jesus' therapeutic tactics show keen awareness of how crowd mentality and cultural conventions—in these cases, I will suggest, a society's sexual conventions—often lead its most vulnerable members to grave psychological and somatic distress.

To recount the narrative, Jesus returns to his native Galilee from Gentile territory only to be greeted by a surging crowd. Jairus, a leader of the local synagogue, falls prostrate and begs Jesus to come to his home to heal his only child, a twelve-year-old daughter who is deathly ill. While Jesus is on his way and still surrounded by throngs of people, a woman who has suffered continual menstrual bleeding for twelve years and is now impoverished from having sought out many physicians to no avail, presses forward to touch the fringe of his robe. As she does so, she senses immediately that the bleeding has stopped, even as Jesus detects some change within himself. He stops to ask who touched him. Peter points out that many have been pressing in. But Jesus dismisses this, saying, "Someone touched me; for I noticed that power had gone out from me." The woman, no longer able to remain anonymous, trembles forward and explains how she came to be healed. Jesus replies, "Daughter, your faith has made you well; go in peace."

Just then, an envoy from the house of Jairus arrives to report that Jairus's daughter has died. Jesus consoles Jairus by saying, "Do not fear. Only believe, and she will be saved." He continues on to the house. When he arrives, he dispels the mourners, for they laugh at him when he tells them that the child "is not dead but sleeping." He allows inside only Peter, John, and James, and the child's parents. He takes the girl's hand and calls out, "Child, get up!" She gets up. He tells the astonished parents to give her something to eat and to tell no one what has happened (see Luke 8:40–56).

All three Synoptic Gospels join in tandem these two healing accounts, which share numerous parallels (Matt. 9:18–26; Mark 5:21–43). Anxious desperation saturates both encounters: Jairus's devastating fear for his child, the woman's intrepid effort to reach Jesus and her consequent alarm in being called out by him from the crowd. The number twelve surfaces both as the age of Jairus's daughter and as the number of years the woman has been suffering. Jesus chooses terms of endearment both for the woman, whom he calls "Daughter," and for Jairus's daughter, whom he addresses as "Child." In both cases, the healing is immediate and embodied; the circumstances of those previously ill are dramatically changed.

Another parallel significant for those of us who minister in this season of justified sensitivity to clergy sexual abuse and of sexual intimacy being mediated electronically through digital proxy[1] is how for Jesus the power of human touch factors into both healings: the woman touches Jesus' cloak; Jesus takes the girl by the hand. Each instance of touch reflects how, to borrow the helpful distinction of psychiatrists Thomas G. Gutheil and Glen O. Gabbard (1993), a boundary crossing need not entail a boundary violation; boundary violations almost always harm, whereas boundary crossings sometimes heal (pp. 188–96; see also Arjona Mejía, 2017). In the biblical examples, each instance of touch signifies a therapeutic boundary crossing, not a boundary violation, but that comes nonetheless at the cost of socially contaminating Jesus: menstruating women in biblical times were

---

1. Richard Kearney (2014), a philosopher at Boston College, recounts conversations with his students about "losing our senses," particularly the sense of touch, in an "increasingly virtual world." His students admit to enjoying the relative anonymity of messaging online "before having 'real contact' with partners," using "acronyms that signaled their level of willingness to have sex, and under what conditions." He notes the paradox in "the ostensible immediacy of sexual contact [being] in fact mediated digitally" and discerns that "what is often thought of as a 'materialist' culture" is "arguably the most 'immaterialist' culture imaginable—vicarious, by proxy, and often voyeuristic" (p. 4SR). While reports on how much of the Internet consists of pornographic material tend to be wildly exaggerated (37 percent is often cited), the best recent empirical data, in Ogas and Gaddam (2012), suggest that about 4 percent of the one million most frequented websites and 14 percent of all web searches are devoted to pornography, though these figures still represent, as Ogas notes (as cited in Ward, 2013), "very significant numbers." Ogas (as cited in Ruvolo, 2011) also points out that "the single most popular adult site in the world is LiveJasmin.com, a webcam site that gets around thirty-two million visitors a month, or almost 2.5 percent" of the world's one billion Internet users. On this site, men pay to watch "women strip on a webcam" while being able to talk with them. Through apps such as Snapchat, Snapcash, and Kik, reports Nick Bilton (2015) in the *New York Times*, targeted virtual sex is now easily accessed on smartphones and will account for $2.8 billion in porn-related revenue in 2015. Why, Bilton asks, would anyone "pay for online pornography when it's available free everywhere"? Because "a private video chat on your mobile phone with a naked person is much more intimate and personal than a website or even a webcam. (So I hear.)" One Snapchat user told him "that people were attracted to the one-on-one nature of the interaction, as well as the built-in privacy." Kari Lerum (as cited in Richtel, 2013), a sociologist at the University of Washington, says that "men are more open, vulnerable and emotional in [web]cam [chat]rooms than in, say, strip clubs. They can also become invested in a relationship that exists only on the screen. 'This is mutual objectification,' she said of camming."

considered ritually unclean, and touching the dead likewise was forbidden (see Schüssler Fiorenza, 1994, p. 124; Green, 1997, pp. 343–44, 350–51; Haber, 2003, pp. 182–83, 187; Kinukawa, 1994, p. 288; Rambo, 2009, pp. 245–46).

The Secret We May not Be Able to Keep

An additional parallel that goes unnoticed by biblical scholars in this striking series of similarities is that the *physical* suffering of both the woman and the girl likely stems from a common *psychological* root or condition, what in biblical times and down through the centuries would have been called *hysteria*, but what today we would diagnose as *somatoform* or *conversion disorders* or, in the newest edition of *The Diagnostic and Statistical Manual of Mental Disorders* (5th ed.; *DSM-5*; American Psychiatric Association, 2013), as *somatic symptom disorders*. The bodily afflictions of the woman and the girl manifest a conflict of mind or soul. To claim that their very real physical symptoms—continual menstrual bleeding in the woman's case, constriction of breathing to the point of appearing dead in the girl's—derive from a psychological source is to say that this woman and this girl are suffering from an inability to express something they desire or, more likely, something they have forgotten they desire.

"Symptoms," Phillips (1995) observes, "are always a self-cure for terror and ecstasy, ways of dosing the intensity of what people feel for, and want from, each other" (p. 45). A symptom "is the secret we may not be able to keep . . . , the sign of a wish to make something known, but by disguising it" (p. 33). At times these symptoms manifest in somatic ways, as in *somatoform disorders*, which can appear as "chronic fatigue, appetite loss, and gastrointestinal and genital-urinary problems," including irregular menses (Capps, 2008, p. 13); or in *conversion disorders*, whereby unconscious psychological conflict becomes symbolically expressed in debilitating neurological disorders such as paralysis, blindness, or even seizures or convulsions (Capps, 2008, pp. 8–9). In such instances, "part of the mind," as British psychoanalyst Nina Coltart (1992) puts it, "has lodged on a psychotic island on the body," and we therefore "have to ask what is the unthinkable content . . . How do we build a bridge which really holds over the secret area of the body-mind divide?" (p. 13). Psychotherapy becomes then in this sense, for Phillips (1995), a way of "trying to remember what you want" (p. 43).

In his book *Jesus the Village Psychiatrist*, Donald Capps (2008) seeks to show that the physical illnesses or disabilities Jesus healed, including those suffered by the woman with the flow of blood and by Jairus's daughter, were typically psychological in origin (pp. xii–xiv). Because Jesus could recognize the nature of these illnesses in his approaches to healing, Capps says, "he was more skilled than the physicians of his day . . . [His methods] were more effective because he had a deeper understanding of how psychosomatic illnesses work and how they affect the person who suffers from them" (p. xiv).

Capps in no way intends to minimize the nature of the actual severe physical distress these individuals experience. The woman and the girl are not in any sense feigning their symptoms nor likely aware of the precipitating psychological conflict. They are not "faking" anything. Neither does his claim diminish the miraculous nature of these healings as marvelous acts of God. There is no shortage of evidence showing that mental illnesses are more intractable and difficult to treat than ones rooted in traceable medical conditions. Many physicians willing to take the money of the hemorrhaging woman were unable to help her.

But Capps *does* suggest that Jesus' miraculous healings did not contradict known scientific laws. Instead, for Capps, "God acted through the deeper knowledge of scientific laws that Jesus brought to his encounters with the sick and disabled" (p. xiv). In the cases of the hemorrhaging woman and of Jairus's daughter, these laws have specifically to do with how, in Coltart's (1992) words, a part of the mind can lodge itself "on a psychotic island on the body" (p. 13).

Capps points out that accounts of so-called hysterias in the ancient world predate the time of Jesus by thousands of years. He cites Mark S. Micale's (1995) history of hysteria, which notes that the ancient Egyptians attributed the condition to an actual free-floating movement, or "wandering," of a woman's uterus within her body, which in turn could lead to respiratory pressure, a loss of voice, or other forms of physical distress. Micale writes, "Egyptian doctors developed an array of medications to combat the disease. Foremost among these measures were the placement of aromatic substances on the vulva to entice the womb back down into its correct position and the swallowing of fetid or foul-tasting substances to repel the uterus away from the upper parts" (Capps, 2008, p. 16; citing Micale, 1995, p. 19).

"The Greeks," Capps continues, "adopted this idea of the migratory uterus and made more explicit the connections between hysteria and an unsatisfactory sexual life" (p. 16). In the fifth century BCE, for example, Hippocrates, the father of Greek medicine, explained "that a mature woman's deprivation of sexual relations causes a restless womb to move upward in search of gratification," leading to "dizziness, motor paralyses, sensory losses, and respiratory distress . . . as well as extravagant emotional behaviors" (Capps, 2008, p. 16; citing Micale, 1995, p. 19). Plato saw the womb as "an animal that longs to generate children" and that therefore becomes especially disturbed "when it remains barren too long after puberty" (Capps, 2008, p. 110; citing Micale, p. 19, quoting *Timaeus*).

Later, as anatomical knowledge grew more refined, Roman physicians abandoned the hypothesis of an actual wandering womb but continued to link hysteria to the female reproductive system or to "diseases of the womb" (Capps, 2008, p. 16; citing Micale, 1995, p. 20). They discovered the condition "most often in virgins, widows, and spinsters," particularly because it was known to begin at puberty and end at menopause (Capps, 2008, p. 110). Capps notes that this would have been the "prevailing medical view" at the time in which Jesus lived.

Capps's conviction—that the woman's continuous menstrual flow and the respiratory diminution of Jairus's daughter derived from psychological sources—may on first hearing disturb persons of faith. But even conservative biblical commentators have long speculated on a psychological origin of the woman's condition in particular, though not that of the girl. In his 1963 commentary on Luke's Gospel, for example, Oxford theologian G. B. Caird (1963) writes that the woman "had an illness (menorrhagia—a continuous menstruation) which was probably psychological in origin, but none the less distressing and debilitating in its effects" (p. 124). He also notes that it rendered her permanently "unclean."

David Lyle Jeffrey (2012), in his commentary on Luke, speculates, "There is a conflict between desire and conscience in the woman" (p. 129). Shelly Rambo (2009) implies that exposure to trauma was the source of the woman's illness. Green (1997) stresses less the psychological origins but more the enormous psychological implications of the woman's condition:

> The simple fact that she is a woman in Palestinian society already
> marks her as one of low status. In addition to this, she was sick,
> and her sickness, while apparently not physically debilitating,
> was socially devastating. Her hemorrhaging rendered her ritually

unclean, so that she lived in a perpetual state of impurity. Although her physical condition was not contagious, her ritual condition was, with the consequence that she had lived in isolation from her community these twelve years . . . The press of the crowds guarantees that she will infect others with her impurity, and her aim to touch Jesus is a premeditated act that will pass her uncleanness on to him . . . This is the story of her resolution to cross the borders of legitimate behavior to gain access to divine power. (pp. 346–47)

Similarly, Hisako Kinukawa (1994) describes the woman's hemorrhaging as "the kind of disease that makes women depressed as well as unhealthy"; she is "polluted," not because of anything she chose, nor because of birth, but due "to the labelling . . . done by those who hold power" (pp. 287–88). Biblical commentators thus surmise both potential psychological origins and inevitable psychological ramifications of the woman's condition.

An Inability to Speak One's Desires

In the case of Jairus's daughter, however, commentators typically assume that, prior to Jesus' arrival in the house, the girl has actually died. This in turn puts even theologically conservative scholars in the awkward position of siding with the very crowd that mocks Jesus for suggesting that the girl is merely sleeping, the only instance in the Gospels in which Jesus is ridiculed in his efforts to heal (Capps, 2008, p. 108). Caird (1963), who as noted allowed that the hemorrhaging woman's condition was likely psychological in origin, maintains in the case of Jairus's daughter that Jesus' "assertion that she was only sleeping was simply an assurance of his unlimited confidence in his own ability to wake her from the sleep of death" (p. 124). Jocelyn McWhirter (2013, p. 52), commenting on the account in Mark's Gospel, notes that "Jesus encounters the corpse surrounded by weeping mourners" and that he, in turn, "commands the dead child to 'get up [egeire].'" Loretta C. Dornisch (2002) says of the crowd that mocks Jesus, "No wonder they ridicule him: They know that she indeed has died" (p. 105). Similarly, Green (1997) writes that "in interpreting the girl's condition as 'sleep' rather than 'death,' [Jesus] has made an authoritative claim that [the crowds] are unwilling to accept. Of course, in an important sense, the crowds speak the truth; the girl's death has already been reported to Jairus (and thus to Luke's audience), and is known by all who have gathered" (pp. 350–51).

But why in this singular instance in the Gospels would faithful believers fail to take Jesus at his word? Why choose instead to side with the very crowd that, as a consequence of its scorn, Jesus throws out of the house (especially evident in Mark 5:39–40)? In their attempt to defend Jesus' capacity to raise the dead, biblical scholars uncharacteristically assume here that Jesus is choosing euphemism over truth.

But Capps (2008), for his part, does take Jesus at his word. If Jesus did not really believe that the girl was sleeping, he writes, "he would seem to be playing with their emotions, a rather inhumane thing to do in the case of death" (p. 108). "In fact," he continues, "it could be argued that if [Jesus] did *not* mean what he said, it is the only statement or comment attributed to him in the Gospels where he affirmed something *that he did not hold to be true*" (p. 122, italics original). Instead, Capps suggests that the girl had a condition that mimicked, as sometimes occurs in somatoform disorders, a "'death-like trance' that could last hours, even days" (Capps, 2008, pp. 111, 113; citing Smith-Rosenberg, 1981, p. 210).

Capps compares her symptoms to those of Alice James (1848–1892), sister of the famous brothers the psychologist William James and novelist Henry James Jr. Alice James thought of herself as a hysteric. Throughout her life as a near invalid she simulated a theatrical "scene of perpetual dying" (Capps, 2008, p. 113; citing Bronfen, 1992, p. 389). Capps notes that at the time of Alice's death in 1892 at age forty-three, Henry, with whom she had been living in England, sent a cablegram to William in Boston to report her death. In his reply, William, "an expert on mental disorders, including hysteria," cautioned Henry "to make sure the death was not only apparent, because her neurotic temperament and chronically reduced vitality are just the field for trance-tricks to play themselves upon" (Capps, 2008, p. 114; citing Bronfen, 1992, p. 391). William, in other words, wanted Henry to be doubly certain that this time their sister really was dead.

Capps (2008, pp. 116–19) finds in the "excessive" nature of the symptoms in the biblical cases of the hemorrhaging woman and Jairus's daughter plausible evidence of a somatoform etiology: "The daughter is near death for no clearly stated reason; the woman's symptoms are far beyond what would appear to be normal, and the effect of seeking treatment for these symptoms has had personal consequences that seem outlandish given the nature of the medical condition itself" (p. 119). If Capps's nuanced analysis is correct, this would suggest that the woman and girl are suffering physically from the incapacity to express some unconscious psychological conflict or desire, or from their inability to speak what they have forgotten they desire. Their symptoms are a self-cure for terror or ecstasy, the sign of a wish to make something known, the secret they are not able to keep. In this case, the inquisitive therapist would be curious to know the actual "unthinkable content" and would want to attend to how in Jesus' healing approach he builds "a bridge which really holds over the secret area of the body-mind divide" (Coltart, 1992, p. 13).

Unthinkable Thoughts

In the chapter titled "Agency and Communion in Human Sexuality" in *The Duality of Human Existence: Isolation and Communion in Western Man*, psychologist David Bakan (1966) defends Freud's emphasis on sexuality as a "touchstone for understanding the nature of [persons]" (p. 102), especially their somatoform symptoms. Writing in the mid-1960s at the height of the sexual revolution, Bakan acknowledges that both anti-Freudians and neo-Freudians express objections "to the significance [Freud] attributed to sexuality," objections based, for example, on the "fact that human beings are concerned with many other [problematic] things" besides sex and on Freud's stressing infantile sexuality rather than sexuality as it emerges in adolescence (pp. 102–3). Bakan posits—correctly, from our current vantage—that these disputes will continue unabated into the future but stakes his claim on Freud's view, given what he considers several "*a priori* bases for the acceptance of the significance of sexuality in human functioning and development" (p. 103). These bases shed light on how, in Coltart's (1992, p. 13) words, part of the mind can so readily lodge on a psychotic island in the body.

First among these foundations for Bakan's (1966) claim that sexuality is a primary path to understanding human nature "is that *sexuality is the function of the human organism . . . most closely related to [an individual's] very existence*" (p. 103, italics original). Freud points out that a child's first mystery is where babies come from; just as the child's question gets to the heart of existence, so sexuality speaks to the heart of the deeper existential riddle: *What is life all about anyhow?* Curiosity about the mysteries of life for children, according to Freud, soon inevitably spills over into sexual curiosity (Bakan, 1966, p. 104).

Bakan's second foundation for asserting sexuality's significance concerns "the mind-body distinction" (p. 105). He notes that many "thought processes, feelings, or wishes take place in the human psyche without any conspicuous changes in the physical operations of the body" and that likewise many changes in the body occur without extensive psychological involvement. When it comes to sexual interests and desires, however, the mind and body are inextricably intertwined: "Thus, for example, the psychological and physiological aspects of sexual arousal correspond so closely that there is little invitation to conceptualize them in terms of any mind-body distinction" (p. 105). In our sexual interests, not unlike in our spiritual ones, body and mind most closely conspire.

Finally, Bakan notes the immense discrepancy between an "overendowment" of human sexual desire and our "underendowed" reproductive potentiality (p. 106). Human sexual capacities and interests far exceed anything necessary to conceive and care for children—evident, for example, in the enormous number and continuous production of sperm cells over the lifetime of males, who can ejaculate many times per week; in the number of ova produced by women, which far exceeds the number of children they can bear; and in the sexual interests of children, including their capacity for orgasm even prior to puberty.

Given these foundational observations—that sexuality pervades our existential questions, bridges the "secret area of the body-mind divide" (Coltart, 1992, p. 13), and is vastly overdetermined in terms of species survival—Bakan finds convincing Freud's radical emphasis on sexuality as a marker for understanding human experience. As an individual's intense sexual interests and anxieties clash with a society's severe sexual conventions, unthinkable psychological content can become symptomatic, lodged on a psychotic island on the body. The task of the therapist becomes one of building a bridge that crosses over the secret area of the body-mind divide.

Believing in Those Who Believe in Us

Returning again to the biblical narratives, the nature of the unthinkable content or conflict is not at all difficult to imagine in the circumstances of a twelve-year-old girl who, as Green (1997) notes, is at the age of puberty and therefore "near the age of betrothal and preparation for marriage" (p. 345; see also Schüssler Fiorenza, 1994, p. 124). Capps (2008) reflects on this widespread societal convention in the ancient world that for many girls must have been—and in more than fifty countries of the world today, for both girls and boys, continues to be (see Sweis, 2014; Strochlic, 2014;

Sinclair, 2015)—its severe psychological repercussions. Jairus's daughter, he writes,

> was at a critical age, expected to become a woman and assume all the responsibilities that womanhood entailed, yet emotionally speaking, she was still a little girl. Confronted with these developmental ambiguities, it would not be surprising if a twelve-year-old girl were to find this a greater challenge than she could handle and fall victim to one or more of the symptoms associated with hysteria. (p. 113)

Her death-like trance, Capps concludes, "suggests that whatever future she expects or anticipates as a sexual being is experienced, unconsciously, as tantamount to death itself." He asks:

> Has the anxiety that underlies her symptoms been aroused by the prospect of having sexual relations with a man she does not respect or love? Or by the prospect of being the mother of children? We cannot know for certain. We may assume, however, that by taking to her bed, and experiencing herself as dying, she was able to keep her psychological conflicts out of conscious awareness, but at enormous cost to one who was on the threshold of young womanhood. (p. 120)

In the case of the hemorrhaging woman, on the other hand, Capps speculates that her symptom suggests a conflict "relating to sexual irregularities and possibly sexual excesses":

> The psychological conflict is unconscious and may therefore have little if anything to do with her actual, real-life sexual history. In fact, her physical complaints may well have resulted in a secondary gain directly related to the primary gain, that of having an explanation for her nonparticipation in the reproductive and maternal activities that were expected of women at the time: the bearing and rearing of children. The excessive loss of blood, however, would also suggest her own depletedness. (p. 120)

Capps concludes, and I concur, that in the cases of both the girl and the woman, anxieties related to traumatic sexual conflicts offer a plausible explanation for their physical symptoms: "Their somatic symptoms reduced the anxiety and kept the conflict itself out of awareness, but the cost was exceedingly high. For both [of them], life itself was a living death" (pp. 120–21).

Jesus recognizes this high cost of what in our own era Erikson (1974) described as "the misplacement of quantities of love and hate" (p. 49; see also Capps, 2008, p. 127) in the hemorrhaging woman's life. Jesus was able to intervene with her and with Jairus's daughter in ways that others of his contemporaries were not, specifically through an embodied exchange of intense physical and relational energy (Rambo, 2009, pp. 245–46; Reid, 1996, p. 140) not unlike what, centuries later, Freud would recognize as *transference*. Specifically for its vivid depiction of the power of transference, Erikson (1974) finds in the healing of the woman "the decisive therapeutic event in the Gospels":

> This story conveys themes which renew their urging presence in each age: There is the assumption of certain quantities lost and regained and with them a quality of wholeness. Jesus, too, notices that a quantity of virtue has passed from him to her—and this as she touched him, and not (according to the age-old technique) as his hand touched her . . . There could be no doubt, then, that it was her faith in his mission that had made her whole. (pp. 48–49)

As Erikson had in the account of Jesus' healing of the woman, so Capps (2008, p. 208) finds evidence of the power of therapeutic transference in the narrative of the twelve-year-old girl, with whom Jesus forges an instant bond. As I noted previously in the Introduction (p. 12), Capps concludes from the biblical account of her healing that

> *we choose life not because we believe in ideas, however compelling these may be, but because we believe in persons, especially those persons who have faith in us.* In the meeting of their hands, Jesus had transferred his faith to [the girl] and had given her faith in the future. For this, she would need adequate nourishment, so his final therapeutic act was to instruct her parents to give her something to eat. (p. 124, italics added)

Jesus heals, in other words, specifically through *our capacity to trust his faith in us as individuals*. But, I would add, he also *tailors* his expression of faith, evident in these two biblical narratives, to unique circumstances of need. A woman excluded from her society is nonetheless persistent and enterprising in "challenging the arbitrary boundaries set by the establishment for its purpose of maintaining the status quo" (Kinukawa, 1994, p. 291). But then, at the very moment she expects to be publicly humiliated for having intentionally contaminated others, including Jesus, she is instead addressed as "Daughter" and epitomized as an exemplar of faith. With this term of endearment, Jesus restores her status in community, even as he affirms her decision to defy that community's social—including, we surmise, its sexual—conventions. He affirms, in other words, her *agency and initiative*.

Another daughter, gravely conflicted about her society's sexual conventions, is likewise renamed by Jesus, in this case as "Child" (see Haber, 2003, p. 188), and thereby is entitled to be served by parents rather than compelled to serve another as wife. In this instance, Jesus expresses his faith in the girl's social subversion by affirming her *passivity and dependence*.

We find in the cases of the woman and the girl, then, that healing occurs through *intense but distinctive exchanges* of transference energy, through their belief in one who believes in them. This mutually empathic belief system is powerful enough to combat severe physical symptoms deriving from a conflict between conscience and desire, symptoms that are "a self-cure for terror and ecstacy . . . , the sign of a wish to make something known" (Phillips, 1995, pp. 33, 45). The woman and the girl are physically ill, their troubled minds having "lodged on a psychotic island on the body" (Coltart, 1992, p. 13), because of social conventions and sexual contradictions they fully inhabit but cannot consciously "think" or know. The crowd mentality isolates them from their feelings or desires. Their sexuality and their loneliness meld perfectly, ruinously, together. In Jesus, however, they find someone in whose faith in them they can believe. More simply, to recall Mark Vonnegut's (2010, p. 66) gut check for distinguishing between medical school applicants, which I discussed in the Introduction (p. 4), they find someone in whose presence they feel less lonely rather than lonelier.

Pastoral Counseling as Social Subversion

C. A. Tripp (2003), a former colleague of pioneer sex researcher Alfred Kinsey, went on to attain his PhD in psychology and to become a psychotherapist in private practice in New York. He was also a respected historian of the life of Abraham Lincoln and created an electronic database of everything of record said by Lincoln or by historians about him—an archive still relied on by serious Lincoln scholars today.

In *The Intimate World of Abraham Lincoln*, a book completed just weeks before his death in 2003, Tripp makes a compelling, point-by-point case that Lincoln was ambisexual or, more likely, gay. He proposes that Lincoln's unorthodox sexuality contributed to his distinctive genius and, more important, that such genius never arises as a product of conventional groupthink or morality but instead, as in Lincoln, in rare individuals compelled to dwell at the social margins:

> The uniformity that every society struggles to maintain for smoothness and easy communication (and in no small measure to defend its dogmas) is precisely the opposite of what genius requires for expression—that is, a freedom from constraint and a degree of wildness that lives at the very edge, or well over the edge, of social value. (p. 210)

Tripp notes that on the surface Lincoln "was quick to support conventional values" and the necessity of obeying the law. His reputation for being ethically above reproach was entirely merited, acknowledged even by his enemies.

But there was another side to Lincoln, Tripp points out, one that was "kind, empathetic, and sympathetic to a fault, with a quick readiness to side with plain folk," even when this involved breaking the rules and cutting through government regulations when necessary: "When it came to his personal judgments he was quite ready to make a mockery of morals, as he often did in his wit; and in serious matters he virtually always came down on the side of comfort and kindness as he placed the personal desires of individuals well ahead of formal regulations of any kind" (p. 210).

Tripp attributes this "two-sidedness" in Lincoln—unimpeachable ethics coupled with unconventional morals—to a lifelong "inversion" or "reversal of commonly expected behavior" (p. 216) derived in part from an ambiguous sexuality that propelled him to the periphery (p. 211). Lincoln's recipe of pliable morality mixed with strenuous ethicality—a sane person, Phillips (2005, p. 199) says, "needs to be able to lie to the Gestapo and tell the truth to one's friend"—strikes me as in keeping with Jesus' healing ethos with the woman and the girl. This combination runs to the heart of what I seek to convey in this chapter, less a plea than an attempt to recognize and applaud what in their vocations ministers who offer effective counsel already know and do. What they in fact do, day after day, is *to host healing conversations that attend to the small differences and the unique interests of individuals who suffer at the periphery as a consequence of crowd mentality.* They listen to that one who confides in them so as to help him or her feel less lonely.

I recall counseling a young seminary student tormented over his sexual longings for other men. He agonized in trying to share with me a specific incident that had occurred only months earlier during his senior year at the conservative Christian college he attended in the South. Entering the college library one day for what he considered routine study and without any overt sense of distress, he sat down at a table and took out a piece of paper. For some unknown reason, however, all at once he found himself overcome by what he knew even at the time was an accumulation of internalized frustration and despair over his inability to free himself of homoerotic desire. Finding himself suddenly in tears there in the library, this upright young man vigorously started writing *Fuck you, Fuck you* over and over again on the page, until a point where his rage turned inward, such that with equal fervor he began writing *Fuck me, Fuck me* again and again instead. Finally, still angry but now exhausted, the paper filled with obscenities, he pulled a random book from the stacks, put the paper inside, and replaced the book on the shelf. The next day, having had second thoughts about someone happening upon that piece of paper in the book, he returned to the library to retrieve it, found the book, but discovered that the paper was already gone.

As the student finished telling of this incident, his head and eyes were downcast with tears of shame. I responded by saying, "It sounds like you were praying." He was not expecting this and lifted his head to search my face, as if to ask, *Are you joking?* I wasn't, and so after a moment I continued, "That may have been your first real prayer. What if you were finally asking God for what you really want? You may have been asking for that much intimacy with God." More stunned silence, then more tears, this time not of agony but of release. At this point in our conversation, it seems pretty safe to suggest, we were both feeling much less lonely.

6

Follow the Naked Christ Naked

Childhood Suffering and the Christian Body

[Jesus] said to them, "Why are you frightened, and why do doubts arise in your hearts? Look at my hands and my feet; see that it is I myself. Touch me and see."

—LUKE 24:38–39A

Perhaps without fully knowing it himself, without full consciousness of multiple potential meanings, he was following the naked Christ naked.

Fred Rogers, the namesake of the beloved PBS children's television program *Mister Rogers' Neighborhood*, appears to have made a point of being seen naked by male journalists who profiled him. Tom Junod (1998), an award-winning journalist for *Esquire* magazine, begins his moving and definitive profile of Mister Rogers, "Can You Say . . . Hero?", with a long description of the then seventy-year-old Rogers as he stripped down to his birthday suit in the locker room of the Pittsburgh Athletic Club, where Rogers swam religiously for thirty minutes each morning at seven o'clock before heading off to his television studio. Rogers would apparently awaken from their slumber those men assigned to interview him so that they might swim with him at the club, and in this exercise he never chose to hide his nakedness from them. To the contrary, as he stands there in the locker room in what Junod describes as his "bobbing-nudity," Rogers says to him in that "voice that sounds adult to the ears of children and childish to the ears of adults . . . , 'Well, Tom, I guess you've already gotten a deeper glimpse into my daily routine than most people have'" (p. 1432). It is pretty clear in these words that Rogers intended to be seen by journalists in all his glory and therefore also, we might conjecture, to be known somehow as fully human, fully male, not just in person but in print, to the public to whom he knew these journalists would report.

It is natural for us to speculate in this about underlying sexual innuendo or yearnings in Rogers, if for no other reason than that we know Mister Rogers was no ordinary man. He once got caught in the rain without an umbrella in New York City and could not find a cab, so he took the subway. The train happened to be crowded with African American and Latinx children who had just been released from school for the day. On seeing Mister Rogers they spontaneously burst into singing "Won't You Be My Neighbor?" right there on the subway car, and because of him and because of them, and despite the downpour outside, a beautiful day it must have been (Junod, 1998). Rogers was no mere mortal, and maybe this was manifested in some hidden way—how could it not have been?—in his sexual yearnings or difference.

I once asked a close friend of Rogers, like Fred also a Presbyterian minister, whether he thought Rogers may have struggled with concerns around sexual identity. The friend told me he had never really thought much about Rogers's sexual ambiguity, though it was certainly possible that this may have been his inner struggle. But the friend added to the chorus of those who have told me that Rogers was completely transparent—that the Mister Rogers one saw on the television show was the same Fred Rogers one met in real life.

Scars with Stories to Tell

My guess instead is that Rogers wanted to show his body to reporters in the locker room not so much out of sexual yearnings, though this too is conceivable, but rather because his body was for him a major wound, a physical scar. His body was his painful scar, and like many of our scars, it revealed, when revealed, an important truth of his life. Our scars have their stories to tell.

Tim Madigan (2006), a reporter who once profiled Mister Rogers for a Fort Worth newspaper and subsequently wrote a book-length biography of him, pointed out, as did Junod, that each day as Rogers got undressed in the locker room, he would weigh himself on a scale. For thirty or more years, Rogers, who was ridiculed for being overweight as a child but grew to be six feet tall and a lean 143 pounds as an adult, refused to eat or do anything that would change that exact number on the scale, including altering the ritualized liturgy of his morning swim (p. 76; see also Junod, 1998).

It is easy to imagine that his naked body signified for him a childhood wound that had become a singular source of that fierce glory he would convey to children in his television show—the message that they are special, that just as those schoolchildren knew spontaneously to sing on the subway, he wants them to be his neighbor. That frail and naked body he compelled those reporters to notice was the fountainhead of the only message that mattered for him as a Christian minister to tell, and still today, in the words of psychologist of religion John McDargh (1995), the answer to the only relevant religious question one can ask: "Does God have regard for me?" "Am I a source of delight to the Source of my delight?" (p. 226). This question, and the answer to it Rogers would offer to children again and again across the years, could only have come to him in the wound that was his very own flesh.

Follow the Naked Christ Naked

Follow the naked Christ naked is an ancient spiritual injunction of monks and mystics dating from the earliest Christian centuries, usually used allegorically and liturgically, as in baptismal rites, but sometimes even literally in ascetic and penitential practices (Jordan, 2003, p. 116, n. 8). It is a precept that may hold continuing intrigue for wounded and wounding churches today.

Christians, however, appear to need to keep the loincloth on Jesus, not so much to protect *him* but, as theological ethicist Mark D. Jordan (2003) claims, "to keep *ourselves* from being ashamed. The cloth covers part of Jesus, which means that it helps us not to look at ourselves" (p. 86, italics added). But ancient Christian forebears urged the faithful to pay attention when Jesus strips down. He is naked in Bethlehem, naked in the Jordan, naked in the Upper Room, naked at Golgotha. Incarnation, baptism, communion, atonement—the major doctrines arrive accompanied by self-exposure, his and, almost certainly, our own. Follow the naked Christ naked.

And Resurrection?

The art historian Leo Steinberg (1996), in his controversial but ultimately stunning achievement *The Sexuality of Christ in Renaissance Art and
in Modern Oblivion*, traces in meticulous detail how Renaissance painters
centered viewers' attention in their pictures specifically on the exposed
genitals of the infant Jesus but also, more startlingly, on the covered but
unmistakably aroused genitals of the risen Christ. Steinberg painstakingly
demonstrates that these Renaissance painters orient our gaze in this way
not out of any newfound imperative for naturalistic painting, nor from
any blasphemous disrespect or pornographic intent. To the contrary, he
concludes, the artists focus on Jesus' nakedness for specifically theological
reasons, namely, in order to depict in scenes of the infant Jesus the full
miracle of God's incarnation in his anatomically correct male body, and to
depict in scenes of the triumphant Jesus' unsubtle arousal the most potent
symbol of resurrection imaginable, if only to men, with no mere substance-
less soul getting raised in this risen Christ.

If one were willing to grant that God is capable of resurrecting someone from the dead—something not always easy to imagine, given how the
dead always in their way persist in death—then it would be easy to imagine
that God is capable of perfecting the resurrected body, one now arriving on
the scene as new and improved, with no flaws, no visible scars, no sign of
wounds.

But this is not at all what one finds in Luke's account of the risen Jesus'
appearances to his friends. Rather, in Luke's Gospel one gets the shamelessly risen Christ of Steinberg's Renaissance painters, a Jesus still somehow
fully embodied, still unquestionably male, and, most stunning of all, still
sporting scars, still bearing wounds. He wants his followers to see them. He
wants them to see *him*. He shows them his wounds.

Those of his friends whose calling would become to report his life
to the world are first going to see his body, Jesus insists, in all its glory, a
glory in this case not in the least sense wispy or ethereal, the way Christians
tend to imagine heavenly bodies and spiritual glory. The risen Jesus' glory
instead arrives in a truly shameful package of apparently shameless glory, a
physical glory, a naked glory, a glory replete with private parts, with frailty
and potency built in, with wounds the source of whatever faith one is finally
to conjure.

"[Jesus] said to them, 'Why are you frightened, and why do doubts
arise in your hearts? Look at my hands and my feet; see that it is I myself.
Touch me and see'" (Luke 24:38–39a). He seeks to mitigate their anxiety

by drawing attention to his body. The risen Jesus has a body like this, like theirs, one scarred and flawed. He points his followers earthward, adjusts their gaze downward, as he was known often to do before. *Look down, look at the children, at the needy, at the marginalized,* he continues to advise even in his glory. *Look at my body, broken for you. Tend to bodies if you would care for souls. Put your ear to other bodies' scars; listen to your own scars, too. Put your hand in my hand, your hand in my side, in these wounds. Touch me and see. This is how one comes to believe, little flock; this is how to believe.* In the resurrection, too, it seems, Jesus strips down once again. He insists on being seen as he is, however fearful his friends may be that in seeing him they themselves might be exposed.

Follow the naked Christ naked advises the ancient injunction. Find in the site of his wounds—and in one's own—the source of God's great triumph.

Meet The Terrible Resistance of Your Childhood Self

British poet laureate and children's book author Ted Hughes, who died in 1998, revealed in an interview (Phillips, 1998, pp. 59–61; citing Heinz, 1995) that he always did his writing in longhand, with a pen, rather than use a typewriter or computer. Writing with a pen, he said, is actually a form of art, for the writer has to *draw* each of the individual letters on the page. Hughes shared a discovery with the interviewer:

> For about thirty years I've been on the judging panel of the W. H. Smith children's writing competition . . . Usually the entries are a page, two pages, three pages . . . Just a poem or a bit of prose, a little longer. But in the early 1980s we suddenly began to get seventy- and eighty-page works. These were usually space fiction, always very inventive and always extraordinarily fluent . . . but without exception strangely boring. It was almost impossible to read them through. [A]s these became more numerous, we realized that this was a new thing. So we enquired. It turned out that these were pieces that children had composed on word processor[s]. What's happening is that as the actual tools for getting words onto the page become more flexible and externalized, the writer can get down almost every thought, or every extension of thought. That ought to be an advantage. But in fact, in all these cases, it just extends everything slightly too much. Every sentence is too long. Everything is taken a bit too far . . . Whereas when writing by hand

you meet the terrible resistance of what happened your first year at
it when you couldn't write at all . . . , when you were making attempts, pretending to form letters. These ancient feelings are there,
wanting to be expressed. When you sit with your pen, every year
of your life is right there, wired into the communication between
your brain and your writing hand. (Phillips, 1998, pp. 60–61; citing Heinz, 1995, italics added)

On a keyboard, Hughes is saying, every letter of the alphabet "feels" exactly
like every other—one fashions an *A* in the very same way one does a *Z*.
Each letter drawn with a pen, by contrast, is necessarily distinct. This physical hardwiring of hand to brain allows to emerge on the page, Hughes says,
the writer's "more compressed . . . [and] psychologically denser" (Phillips,
1998, p. 61; citing Heinz, 1995) struggles of childhood, struggles that long
to be expressed.[1] If somehow we remain in touch with suffering we experienced as children, Hughes implies, our stories become less boring and
rambling, more honest and alive. The challenges and struggles of our childhood pasts are essential to telling the most honest and important stories of
our lives, the path to experiencing God as no longer hidden. Our scars have
their stories to tell.

In personally having taught by now perhaps thousands of seminarians
in scores of courses on pastoral care and counseling, there is invariably one
key message I want them to receive: *Write your life story with a pen, not with
a computer; meet the terrible resistance of your childhood self if in search of
the living Lord.*

Reframing Childhood Wounds

Finnish child psychiatrist Ben Furman (Furman and Ahola, 1992) tells the
story of a woman named Flora referred to him "because of her depression

1. Two decades after Hughes's observations, at a time when Common Core edu-
cational standards now emphasize keyboarding over handwriting after the first grade,
psychologists appear to confirm his insights. Karin James (Konnikova, 2014) of Indiana
University has found that when children draw a letter freehand, rather than trace it or
type it on a keyboard, they activate three areas of the brain that adults activate in reading
and writing. "'When a kid produces a messy letter,' Dr. James said, 'that might help him
learn it.'" Princeton psychologist Pam A. Mueller has demonstrated that "students learn
better when they take notes by hand than when they type on a keyboard. . . . Writing
by hand [allows] the student to process a lecture's contents and reframe it—a process of
reflection and manipulation that can lead to better understanding and memory encod-
ing" (Konnikova, 2014).

and constant weeping" (p. 24). She reported many problems, all of them related to her ex-husband and her two sons. But she was successful in her professional life, where she was known for her talent in drawing out the creativity of children. She told Furman about her past, including one secret from her childhood that she had never shared with anyone else:

> With tears running down her cheeks she revealed that when her mother was drunk she used to shut [Flora] in a dark cupboard for long periods of time. [Furman] sympathized with her and asked, "What did you do there in that dark cupboard? How did you pass the time?" With a miserable look on her face she explained that she used to make up all kinds of imaginary creatures to play with. "How wonderful," [Furman] said. "Do you think that perhaps what you used to do in the cupboard is responsible for the skill you now have with children?" Flora laughed through her tears as she suddenly became able to see her past [suffering] in this light. (p. 24)

Permission to Feel Bad and Sad

Amy Hollingsworth (2005) reveals in another biography of Fred Rogers a time when as a shy, overweight eight-year-old boy he was a regular target of bullies at school. The bullying was so severe that he was usually driven by car to and from school each day. One day when he had to walk home instead, a group of boys followed him, taunting him by calling him "Fat Freddy" and telling him that they were going to get him. He started walking more quickly and knew that "if he could get to the home of a family friend, a widow named Mrs. Stewart, who lived nearby, he could find refuge. While the bullies kept taunting," Hollingsworth writes, "he silently prayed that she would be at home. He banged on the door, and Mrs. Stewart swung it open to let him in" (p. 125).

Rogers said, "I cried to myself [as a child] whenever I was alone . . . I cried through my fingers as I made up songs on the piano. I sought out stories of other people who were poor in spirit, and I felt for them." Adults told him to shrug off the bullies, not to let on to them that he cared. "But even as a child," he said, he "knew that wasn't the answer: 'I resented the teasing. I resented the pain. I resented those kids for not seeing beyond my fatness or my shyness,' and he longed for someone to tell him it was okay to feel that way," that "it was okay to feel bad about what happened, and even to feel sad" (pp. 125–26). But no one did.

Looking back on the childhood bullying he suffered, Rogers counted that period as pivotal and said that these incidents of shame and sadness, rather than leading him to become a bully himself, led him instead to begin, in his words, "a lifelong search for what is essential, what it is about my neighbor that doesn't meet the eye . . . The tough times I've been through . . . turned out to be times in which God's presence was so clear—so real that it felt like Mrs. Stewart opening her door and taking me into her safe home" (p. 126). His willingness as an adult to cross so many borders to reach "the least of these," Hollingsworth concludes, "arose from the realization that he was one of them" (p. 126).

The fact that as an adult Rogers insisted on weighing in on the scale every day at a diminutive 143 pounds suggests to me that those childhood bullies' voices were never fully quieted within him. The wounds they inflicted would remain.

Equally clear to me, however, is that by insisting that those reporters whose calling was to tell Rogers's life to the world see his body in all its naked glory, even its most private parts, Rogers was proclaiming that the bullies would not prevail; that Mrs. Stewart happens to be home just now; that death has lost its sting; that all children of God are a source of delight to the Source of their delight; that in meeting the terrible resistance of one's childhood self by attending to these wounds—one's own and those of Jesus—is God finally known.

A Robed Curate

In 1992, Mister Rogers received an honorary doctorate, his twenty-fifth, this one from Boston University. He was to open the commencement ceremony with prayer. Hollingsworth (2005) describes the mayhem deriving from the presence of this slight man:

> An older academic with a white beard rose to the podium to announce: "The invocation will now be delivered by Mister Fred Rogers." Before he could finish, the five thousand graduates went wild, whooping and hollering out the name of the man they had grown up with, the man whose daily visits convinced them they were "special." When Fred reached the podium, the tumult started again, cameras flashing throughout the crowd. How would he ever

calm them down enough to pray? The answer seemed like the natural thing to do (to Fred at least). He leaned sheepishly into the mike and said, "You wanna sing with me?" And then chiding ever so slightly, "Why don't you just sit down, and we'll sing this song together." And together he and his legion of television neighbors began to sing—in perfect unison, because they all remembered the words, "It's a Beautiful Day in the Neighborhood." Waves of red robes swayed side to side, arms intertwined, subdued by the sense of security and ritual that Mister Rogers had always given them. He was their robed curate, and their congregational response, uplifting and reminiscent, led right into prayer. (pp. 21–22)

7

Wedding of the Waters

Reflections on the Lost and Found Self

To reflect at any length on the nature or experience of the *self*, or on its close companions of *heart, mind, soul,* or *spirit,* is to toy with madness. On close scrutiny the expression *I haven't been myself lately* and other equally commonplace references to the self reveal a bewildering web of thought, feeling, language, and relationship: *Who* hasn't been *what* self lately? How can I *not* be myself? Who is talking about what here? A carnival house of mirrors, a dog chasing its tail—the subjective self becomes inevitably confused and contorted in its attempts to objectify itself. It begins to murmur to itself, to run into itself, to avoid itself, or to exhaust itself. The self experienced as intimately near proves itself likewise to be infinitely far.

The search for the familiar mystery of self spans the centuries and continues unabated today, raising the question of what propels the self into this unceasing investigation. Do we, like proverbial mountain climbers, attempt to scale the self simply because it is *there* (or perhaps more accurately because the self is at once *there* and beguilingly *not* there)? Is there an urgency to such an inquiry beyond the mere challenge to intellectual prowess or stamina? What finally is at stake in this relentless seeking after self by the self?

As I have noted in previous chapters, psychologist of religion John McDargh (1995), quoting the Benedictine monk Dom Sebastian Moore, hints at a promising initial response to such questions in suggesting that the "primary and irreducible proposition about human beings . . . is that 'we all desire to be desired by the one we desire.'" Moore writes, "The only serious form of the religious question today is: Is human self-awareness, when it finds its fulfillment in love, resonating, albeit faintly, with an origin that 'behaves,' infinitely and all-constitutingly, as love behaves?" McDargh continues, "To ask this question in the poetry of the biblical tradition, 'Does God have regard for me?' or 'Am I a source of delight to the Source of my delight?'" (p. 226)

At the heart of the urgent quest for self, McDargh implies, is a yearning for assurance concerning one's status before God, a hunger conveyed primarily through the language of poetry. Incapable of observing or communicating itself directly, the observing and communicating self instead expresses its desires to know and to be known through analogy, metaphor, story, or parable—a poetry no less evident in psychological and social scientific theories of the self than in biblical and theological anthropology.

Wedding of the Waters

In my own reflections on the self, I found my imagination drawing back to some days a number of years ago that I spent on the Amazon river in Brazil. There, near the interior port city of Manaus, I witnessed a geographic wonder known locally as the "wedding of the waters," a convergence of two vast rivers that together form the oceanic Amazon for its final thousand-mile journey to the sea. The waters of the tributary rivers—one the Rio Negro or Black River, and the other an extension of the Peruvian Amazon called in Brazil the Rio Solimões—differ dramatically in color. The Rio Negro, a "black water" river, is sparklingly transparent and free of silt but the color of strong tea, evident even in filling a small glass with its water. The "white" water of the Rio Solimões, by contrast, is actually a muddy brown in color and full of alluvial matter. As these two massive rivers merge, their two colors of water begin to flow side-by-side along a distinct but shifting front, with additional visible patches of black water within white and of white water within black variously interspersed, until eventually the colors thoroughly mix some ten to fifteen miles farther downstream. My eyes appeared to be deceiving me as our boat crossed the unmistakable line from one color of water to the other, but my photographs later confirmed the stunning divide.

This image offers a potentially suggestive metaphor for the self as a particular person's experience at that dramatic yet permeable frontier, that space between worlds, where converge vast but distinctive rivers of body and soul, of finite and transcendent, of consciousness and the unconscious, of individual and other. The self is that boundary experience where these discrete yet fluid edges clash, comingle, and farther downstream eventually, perhaps eschatologically, unite as one.

Not unlike the life of the self it seeks to understand and to assist, the discipline of pastoral theology labors at that liminal place where vastly different streams of thought, belief, experience, and practice clash and converge. It navigates distinctive but shifting boundaries between psychology and theology, between human experience and divine revelation, and between existential urgency and conceptual abstraction. Pastoral theological investigation of the self thus becomes a doubly precarious exercise at the boundary of a boundary, at the edge of a limit experience.

In her study of cultural collisions between understandings of health and illness of Hmong immigrants to the United States and those of Western medicine, journalist Anne Fadiman (1997) captures something of the pastoral theologian's similar vocational interest in life at the boundaries: "I have always felt that the action most worth watching is not at the center of things but where the edges meet. I like shorelines, weather fronts, international borders. There are interesting frictions and incongruities in these places, and often, if you stand at the point of tangency, you can see both sides better than if you were in the middle of either one" (p. x) To speak of the self is to consider another such place where the edges meet and where, like Fadiman, the pastoral theologian finds the action most worth watching. Pastoral theology becomes here our point of tangency—our little boat—from which to witness the frictions, the incongruities, and on occasion the satisfying convergences.

Whatever abstract tenets emerge, then, from a pastoral theological exploration of the self stand in necessary tension with the pressing concerns of particular persons who struggle with debilitating self-depletion and who wonder, *Does God have regard for me? Am I a source of delight to the Source of my delight?* That affirmative answers to these questions remain in grave doubt for countless contemporary persons within and outside the church fuels our continuing search for the elusive self and for the sources of its confusion and redemption.

In this chapter I center this search in Jesus' startling depiction of the "wedding" of self in relation to God in his parables of the lost-and-found sheep, coin, and sons of Luke 15, building here on the exegesis of these parables by Kenneth E. Bailey, a biblical theologian from the United States immersed in Middle Eastern culture. I then consider the influential self psychology of Heinz Kohut, a psychoanalyst who also labored at cultural and disciplinary boundaries. Kohut conceived of the self as a convergence of one's desires and one's ideals and explored tensions between narcissistic self-love and love for others. Finally, I attempt a meeting at those edges demarcating these biblical and psychological depictions of the self by returning to my initial mediating metaphor of the wedding of the waters.

The Lost-and-Found Self of Luke 15

A reproduction of a painting titled *The Forgiving Father* by Frank Wesley (1923–2002), an artist from India who studied in Japan, hangs on the wall of my study, depicting its own sort of powerful convergence. Two men stand against an airy background, the elder embracing the younger. Pathos and passion abound, a remarkable artistic achievement given that viewers who observe this reunion see neither man's face. The bald elder man, draped in an elegant robe, presses his face into the chest of the emaciated, half-naked younger man, the latter's body limp and his own head and hair falling heavily into the father's hand. Like the distinctive colors of the Amazon's waters, the son's ashen gray skin sharply contrasts with the vital brown flesh of his father. Like the wedding of the waters, on the right side of the painting distinctive lines of color clearly differentiate the father both from the background and from his son, suggesting immanence and individuation; whereas on the left side the pink robe of the father blends seamlessly into the celestial pink background as well as into the son's own cloth wrap, suggesting transcendence and communion.

I once showed this painting to Kenneth E. Bailey (1930–2016), who was a visiting professor at the seminary where I was then teaching. An evangelical New Testament scholar and expert linguist with a classical Western education, Bailey had spent several decades teaching in the Arabic language in the Middle East, much of that time engaged in studying the parables of Luke 15. He commented on the poignancy of the painting but then suggested that its one shortcoming was its failure to depict the crowd of people from the tightly-knit Middle Eastern village that would have played witness to this father's stunning embrace, and whose implied presence in Jesus' parable of the prodigal son heightens its convictional power. Somewhat disheartened by Bailey's response, given my almost visceral connection to the painting, I did not think to suggest that perhaps the artist intended that those who view the painting should stand in place of the village crowd. Bailey's critique of the painting stemmed, however, from his fundamental conviction that the parables of Jesus, like contemporary political cartoons, cannot be fully understood apart from the nuances of the culture in which they originated.

In his book *Finding the Lost: Cultural Keys to Luke 15*, Bailey (1992, p. 49) describes his own intellectual and theological pilgrimage that resulted from his professional work at a point of cultural tangency between East and West. While Western education fostered in him the primacy of conceptual abstraction and academic dispassion, Bailey found to his surprise in the Middle East that metaphor, parable, and intensity of feeling took precedence over conceptual interpretation at even the highest levels of scholarship and society. Jesus, who in Bailey's Western way of thinking exemplified a simple and ethical carpenter but not a rigorous intellectual or theologian, was recognized by Jesus' own contemporaries, Bailey came to realize, as one unreservedly worthy of the deferential title of rabbi and as one whose theological teaching—in parables—astonished his hearers.

Since metaphorical theology like that of Jesus' parables builds on the stuff of ordinary life from a particular culture, Bailey became convinced that a keen understanding of that original cultural climate was essential for its interpretation:

> If theology is composed with philosophy at its base, then training in that philosophy is all that one needs to pursue that theology. But if theology is created by simile, metaphor, parable, and dramatic action, then the culture of the theologian and his/her people is a critical key for unlocking the theological intent of the metaphorical language . . . Having struggled for more than a generation with this problem in both the East and the West, it is my perception that for us as Westerners the cultural distance "over" to the Middle East is greater than the distance "back" to the first century. The cultural gulf between the West and the East is deeper and wider than the gulf between the first century (in the Middle East) and the contemporary conservative Middle Eastern village. (pp. 28–29)

Bailey attempts to bridge this cultural divide in interpreting what are arguably Jesus' most influential depictions of the self in relation to God—the parables of the lost sheep, the lost coin, and the lost sons of Luke 15.

Although he sees nothing improper in the Western propensity to squeeze abstract concepts from metaphors or parables, just as there is nothing improper about squeezing juice from an orange, Bailey nonetheless maintains that the whole of the metaphor, like the whole of the orange, resonates at a deeper personal level than does any condensation or abstraction. This leads him to speculate on the self's own metaphoric constitution: "We are body and mind/spirit, held together in a mysterious 'solution' that none can understand. Even so, the metaphor combines a concrete base in the physical world that can be seen and touched and felt with an unseen spiritual reality. Thus the metaphor speaks to the whole person in a way that concept does not" (p. 19). To suggest, as Bailey does here, that the self functions like a metaphor—as a conduit between the physical and the spiritual—is to argue that the self is *like a likeness* or *analogous to an analogy*, a quandary that further underscores the self's characteristic elusiveness.

The Acceptance of Being Found

What, then, can one learn of the self from a culturally sensitive reading of Jesus' familiar parables of the lost sheep, coin, and sons? Bailey begins by noting that all three parables are set in Luke's Gospel in a context of controversy surrounding Jesus' table fellowship: *Now all the tax collectors and sinners were coming near to listen to [Jesus]. And the Pharisees and the scribes were grumbling and saying, "This fellow welcomes sinners and eats with them"* (Luke 15:1–2). Jesus doubly offended the religious establishment, Luke indicates, by eating with persons tainted under Jewish ceremonial purification laws and with those hated for collaborating with the foreign occupying government. Bailey (1992, pp. 61–62) suggests that "for both Jesus and for the Pharisees, table fellowship (or lack thereof) was a critical symbol of identity" and therefore, I would add, a promising symbol of the self. Jesus responds to the Pharisees' objections not with a conceptually argued defense but by telling stories, each one ending, significantly, with an image of a celebratory gathering or meal.

The parables of Jesus, Bailey asserts, lend themselves to multiple but not unlimited levels of interpretation. They can be understood as entertaining stories enjoyable to "children" of all ages; as ethical teachings that suggest patterns of conduct to emulate or to avoid; more important, as theological revelations of the secrets of God; and in some cases as indirect expressions of Jesus' own christological self-understanding (p. 50). Regarding this latter purpose, some commentators suggest that the parables of Luke 15 in particular lack any evidence of a mediator between God and humanity, thereby diminishing their christological significance. Bailey argues to the contrary, however, that their christological claims are established from the very outset; the Pharisees charge that Jesus welcomes sinners and eats with them, and Jesus responds by telling stories of a shepherd, a woman, and especially a father who do precisely what Jesus himself is accused of doing (pp. 62–63).

Recall that in the first of these parables a shepherd loses one of his one hundred sheep, leaves the ninety-nine in the wilderness to search out the lost, and on finding it lays it on his shoulders and returns home, imploring his friends to join in celebrating his accomplishment. In the second, a woman with household fiduciary responsibilities loses a substantial coin and lights a lamp by which to search for it; when she finds it, she too gathers her friends and neighbors, asking them to rejoice with her for having found the lost coin. In the third parable, the younger of a wealthy landowner's two sons asks for his share of the inheritance; the father divides his estate between the sons, whereupon the younger one squanders his portion in reckless living in a distant country. After suffering a famine there he returns home seeking to persuade his father to take him in as a paid craftsman, but the father instead rejoices that his son has been found and insists on a lavish banquet celebration. On hearing the festivities from the field, the elder son discovers what has happened and rages against his father for having restored the younger son; the father comes out again, reassures the older son of his steadfast love, but then pleads with him to join the party. Jesus concludes the parables by telling his listeners, explicitly at the end of each of the first two and implicitly in the third, of a great joy in heaven over even one sinner who repents.

These parables depict victimization, sin, and the condition of being "lost," as well as repentance, redemption, and the hope of being "found," themes also keenly relevant to a search for the self. The sheep, the coin, and the two sons all find themselves thoroughly lost in these parables but hold differing degrees of responsibility for their present circumstances. Certainly the coin, Bailey notes, can in no way be held culpable for its fate, a passive "victim" lost through no fault of its own; the sheep, on the other hand, contributes to its own predicament, a victim at least in part of its own stupidity or animal instincts, although the shepherd ultimately must account for its loss. In stark contrast to the coin or the sheep, however, the sons of the final parable carry the full burden of responsibility for their desolation, Bailey insists, as they purposely shame and attempt to sever ties with their father (pp. 67, 103, and in personal communication with author). These parables, then, may be collectively taken to suggest that disparate factors—including victimization, ignorance or indifference, and personal malice—contribute to the depletion or loss of self.

The parables prove decidedly univocal, however, in describing the helplessness of the self in coming to be found. Bailey tells, for example, of how a lost sheep becomes paralyzed by fear, unable even to be compelled to move by the shepherd; the shepherd instead must carry the sheep, which can weigh seventy pounds, over rugged terrain to safety (p. 74). Neither does the lost coin contribute in any way to its coming to be found. Bailey finds this passivity revealing, especially given Jesus' emphasis on repentance at the conclusion of each parable. In likening the acquiescence of the sheep and the coin to repentance, Jesus radically redefines the term: "For Jesus," Bailey writes, "repentance means *acceptance of being found*" (p. 85, italics original). The self contributes to its rescue specifically in the sense of yielding to its rescuer.

What, then, of the lost sons? A lost sheep, after all, is just an animal, a lost coin an inanimate object. But does not the parable of the lost sons, at least, allow for persons to participate more purposefully in their repentance? Bailey responds with a decisive *no* that again arises from his unique cultural location. Western commentators, he asserts, generally gloss over what Middle Eastern commentators universally recognize as the deeply offensive actions of the sons in this parable. By requesting his share of the inheritance before the father has died, the younger son in effect tells his father to drop dead. Such disrespect from a son in a Middle Eastern patriarchal village, Bailey notes, would lead not only to his being considered dead to the family but to his being exiled from the larger community; a Middle Eastern father in this circumstance would be "expected to refuse and drive the boy out of the house with verbal if not physical blows" (p. 112). Western commentators, however, assume that the son's scandalous request is somehow typical of that culture and thereby diminish the stunning magnitude of the father's response in actually granting the request and in suffering the agony of rejected love. Bailey speculates on Jesus' theological motive for depicting the father in this way: "On three different occasions the father in this parable clearly violates the traditional expectations of a Middle Eastern father. This is the first of them. An awareness of the redefinition of the word *father* that takes place in this story is critical for the theology of Jesus in general and for the theological content of this parable in particular" (p.

114). Jesus dramatically portrays here what he has in mind in routinely addressing God as Father, redefining fatherhood not according to the assumptions of Middle Eastern patriarchy but in more feminine, maternal, or transgendered terms.

The father in this parable is a wealthy landowner with servants, paid craftspeople, and livestock. The younger son acts in an outrageous fashion a second time by quickly liquefying his assets, likely selling his share of the father's property to another resident of the small village and thus insulting his father publicly by making known the terrible rupture in the family. The son receives enough money from the considerable estate to journey to a far country for a long period of time. A famine, Bailey points out, does not take its toll overnight.

Given the importance in the Middle East of protecting one's honor and of avoiding shame, the son refrains from returning home after depleting his vast wealth. To go home would be to return to his father as a failure and to live at his brother's expense, since his brother now held all that remained of the estate. In addition, Bailey notes, the prodigal knew that he would find himself ostracized by the entire village for what he had done. So instead of returning home, he takes a job feeding pigs, longing himself to eat what he was feeding them.

We reach here another critical impasse in the interpretation of this parable, the point where the prodigal *came to himself* and returned to his father's home. Does not this decision to return contradict the passive nature of repentance depicted in the previous two parables? Bailey argues to the contrary that his "coming to himself" in no way implies that the son has suddenly repented of his past misdeeds; rather, he has lighted on yet another scheme by which to use his father to save face in his family and community. He decides to "work" his father a bit until the son can convince him to hire him as one of the father's skilled craftspeople but *not*, Bailey notices, as one of the father's unpaid slaves or servants. The son hopes to earn back status in his father's household but without any sense of remorse for his previous actions. Bailey writes, "[The son] has not yet given up. There is one card left in his hand. He hopes it will be an ace" (p. 129).[1]

The father, however, completely undermines the son's carefully laid plan. He again forsakes patriarchal custom and dignity, this time by picking

---

1. Lukan scholar Joel B. Green (1997, p. 581, n. 235) challenges Bailey on this point, finding instead that "shades of repentance are clearly evident" in the younger son's actions.

up the hem of his robe and running through the gauntlet of the narrow village streets in order to greet his son *while he was still far off*. The father interrupts and renders irrelevant the son's rehearsed appeal with a compassionate embrace and with kisses, lavishing on the son symbols of honor (the father's best robe), trust (a signet ring?), and self-respect (sandals) before the disheveled son is seen by the villagers, who now in turn will accept the son out of respect for the father (p. 155).[2] The father's deep compassion overwhelms the prodigal's futile attempt to restore himself:

> The prodigal returns home planning to save himself by his labor as a craftsman. If he is allowed to proceed with his plan, there will be no authentic reconciliation, for any genuine reconciliation will require the prodigal's awareness of the real meaning of what he has done. Only when that awareness dawns on him will he be able to see that he *cannot* solve the problem he has created. The very assumption that he can pay money and compensate for the agony of rejected love is to cheapen the reality of that pain. A broken window is not like a broken heart . . . Genuine reconciliation can only be achieved by the father's self-emptying costly love. (p. 149)

Reclaiming the Unadorned Self

Bailey likens the impact of this father's disarming actions to pastoral theologian Henri J. M. Nouwen's account of leaving prestigious teaching posts to minister to persons with intellectual disabilities who understood nothing of his books or credentials. Nouwen wrote: "These broken, wounded, and completely unpretentious people forced me to let go of my relevant self—the self that can do things, show things, prove things, build things—and forced me to reclaim that unadorned self in which I am completely vulnerable, open to receive and give love regardless of my accomplishments" (Bailey, 1992, p. 154; citing Nouwen, 1990, pp. 15–16). The father's embrace compelled the prodigal to relinquish precisely this relevant self. In this way, Bailey asserts, Jesus continues to characterize repentance, as in the previous parables, as a process of accepting one's being found, of reclaiming one's

---

2. In suggesting that the father runs to clothe and restore the son in part to protect the son's dignity before the villagers see him, Bailey seems to contradict his critical comments concerning the absence of the village crowd in the Wesley painting of this scene that hangs on my wall.

unadorned self. The prodigal's restoration to sonship cannot be earned but instead only conferred by the father's costly love.

This emphasis continues as well in the second part of the parable. A servant tells the elder brother that his father has *recovered* (not merely *received*) his younger brother. The elder brother's ensuing rage would have brought the banquet to a standstill, Bailey claims, as word quickly circulated of the crisis generated by his refusal to participate. In that cultural context his defiance of the father would have been considered more disgraceful than even the unthinkable earlier demands of the younger son, particularly since the elder son's challenge was issued at a public gathering. It takes two hundred people, Bailey points out, to eat a fatted calf (pp. 155, 171).

Here, the father responds for the third time in the story in an unconventional way. He again goes out to meet a thankless son and to absorb his venomous accusations (*I have slaved for you*, the son fumes). Again the father swallows his public honor and responds not with legitimate outrage or with culturally sanctioned violence but with painfully tender reassurances and a plea that this son also would join him at table: *Beloved son, you are always with me, and all that is mine is yours. [But] to celebrate and rejoice was necessary, for this your brother was dead and has come to life; he was lost and has been found* (Luke 15:31–32; Bailey, 1992, pp. 183, 185). The father extends grace *before* the elder son acknowledges any sin, a costly love offered to cover this lost law-keeping son (perhaps personifying the scribes and Pharisees to whom Jesus tells this story) even as grace had been given to cover the lost law-breaking son (perhaps signifying the tax collectors and sinners with whom Jesus eats). The hushed banquet crowd awaits the elder son's reply as the story ends unfinished.

Bailey underscores that the older brother misreads the nature of the banquet celebration. Countering the assumption that the banquet was intended to honor the prodigal, Bailey asserts instead that the *father* and what the father has done are the foci of this revelry. This interpretation is in keeping with both previous parables, in which the shepherd and the woman call together friends and neighbors not for the sake of the sheep or the coin but for their having personally succeeded in finding what they were responsible for having lost. The integrity and diligence of the shepherd, the woman, and now the father who have restored the lost prompt these celebrations (pp. 77–80, 104).

Unlike Western Christians, Bailey notes, Middle Eastern Christians find nothing ignoble in the corresponding image of a self-satisfied God—a

God who saves and rescues the lost not merely for their sake but also for God's own sake, for the sake of God's righteousness and reputation. These parables thus subtly affirm the necessity of self-esteem in relation to the demanding risks of loving and searching out lost others (pp. 79–80). Abounding in unrequited love, the shepherd, the woman, and the father nonetheless express no hesitation in calling for communal admiration of what they alone have accomplished.

Jesus perceives the self, then, according to Bailey's station at the convergence of cultures of East and West, as at once far more helpless and depraved and also more fervently sought and esteemed, as well as more relationally conceived and redeemed, than Western interpretations have tended to concede. If the self is itself a parable of sorts that attempts to wed the concrete physical world to an unseen spiritual reality, and if the self thereby wonders above all, *Does God have regard for me?*—then Jesus responds, in Bailey's reading of Luke 15, with no less than a resounding *yes.* Jesus demonstrates there the depths of God's costly love and satisfaction in finding and welcoming the lost to the banquet table. His unqualified affirmation of God's generous regard for the self appears especially remarkable given his unflinching portrayal of the depths of human isolation and malice—the self lost at times through no fault of its own, lost at other times through its own narcissistic strivings, but hopelessly lost nonetheless.

Key aspects of Bailey's depiction of Jesus' understanding, however, appear to be quite compatible with certain contemporary psychoanalytic assumptions concerning the self, especially constructs found in Kohut's self psychology.

Self Psychology and the Transformation of Narcissism

In 1940, at twenty-seven, Heinz Kohut (1913–1981), the son of a Jewish physician and himself a recent medical school graduate, emigrated under Nazi threat from his native Vienna to the United States. After completing his training in neurology and psychiatry at the University of Chicago Medical School, Kohut remained there and at the Chicago Institute for Psychoanalysis as a professor and clinician until his death in 1981. He found acclaim in psychoanalytic circles in the 1960s and 1970s for his clinical competence with patients suffering from self disorders and for his challenges to psychoanalytic orthodoxy in a series of progressively bold writings. Although schooled in classical psychoanalysis in Chicago and holding Freud in high esteem, Kohut found it increasingly difficult to reconcile Freudian theory with the severity of the psychological dilemmas his patients were facing. He viewed his theoretical and clinical work initially as supplementing, but eventually as supplanting, Freudian psychosexual theory (Kohut, 1984, p. 87; see also pp. 41, 53, 95, 113). Some critics have tended to consider Kohut's claims extreme, but his self psychology continues to retain influence in the United States today (Rangell, 1982, pp. 863–91; Cooper & Randall, 2011).

At issue in this controversy was how best to assist patients diagnosed with narcissistic personality disorders, a psychiatric designation derived from the ancient myth of Narcissus, the tale of a handsome youth who in rejecting the affections of a nymph was condemned by the gods to fall in love with his own ephemeral reflection in a clear mountain pool and thereby to experience the pangs of unrequited love. Freud considered pathological narcissism to be a rare and somewhat severe form of psychological regression. He refused psychoanalytic treatment for persons with narcissistic self disorders, since by definition they could not form significant relationships with other persons, including the "transference" relationship with an analyst necessary for healing in psychoanalytic therapy (Stone, 1986, pp. 1–13, 45–53, 149–58, 411–32).

In mid-twentieth-century Chicago, however, Kohut became perplexed by the disproportionate number of patients who sought psychotherapy for narcissistic symptoms. Freud's patients had suffered from so-called classical neuroses, including phobias, compulsions, or other expressions of anxiety over sexual or aggressive desires that transgressed scrupulously held beliefs and values. Kohut's patients, by contrast, possessed an only sporadically influential conscience or belief system and expressed instead ill-defined complaints related to more fundamental insufficiencies in self-structure— a sense of "falling apart," self-disintegration, depletion, or fragmentation. Most problematic were their dramatic fluctuations in self-esteem along a vast spectrum from extreme grandiosity to severe shame (Kohut, 1971, pp. 16–23).[3] In Kohut's clinical practice, patients exhibiting these more devel-

---

3. See also Dykstra, 1997, p. 55: "They struggled with deep feelings of emptiness and isolation and compensated with grandiose self-inflation or with fantasies of merging with powerfully idealized others. Equally evident were wide pendulum swings to caustic deflation of self and others. Their frantic sexual expressions served to sustain the self but were manipulative of others, characterized by exhibitionism, voyeurism, fetishes, or fantasies of violence in sexual relations. They sensed little continuity, vigor, balance, or direction in their lives and seemed only a crisis or two removed from a chaotic emotional break with reality."

opmentally archaic and intractable narcissistic patterns were becoming the norm rather than the exception.

Unlike Freud, however, Kohut believed that such patients could and indeed would form a transference relationship with the therapist, although a relationship of a unique kind that he called a narcissistic or "selfobject" transference (Kohut, 1984, pp. 192–210). Whereas therapeutic relationships with patients struggling with less severe neurotic symptoms, like most significant relationships, accrued emotional intensity only over a considerable period of time, Kohut found that in patients with narcissistic disorders such intensity of feeling developed with peculiar speed, indeed almost immediately, usually from his very first encounter with them. This highly charged but fragile bond was experienced as a "relationship," however, solely by the patient. In order to bolster a disintegrating sense of self, the patient used the therapist, although without malicious intent, not as an actual psychoanalytic "object," that is, not as an idiosyncratic person in the therapist's own right, but rather as a "selfobject," as if the therapist was merely an extension of the patient's own body. If the therapist refused to be manipulated or objectified in this way, the narcissistic patient's reaction, again from the very outset, was one either of intense rage or shame (Kohut, 1978, pp. 637ff.)

Seeking Acceptance, Merging with Greatness, and Cherishing Camaraderie

Kohut came to recognize that these instant, intensive narcissistic transferences fell into three distinguishable but overlapping patterns that he called the *mirror transference*, the *idealizing transference*, and the *twinship* or *alter ego* transference. In the mirror transference, as its name suggests, the patient unconsciously demands that the therapist function for a considerable time solely as the reflecting pond in the Narcissus myth; the patient tolerates only soothing and affirming mirroring and idealization from the therapist. In the idealizing transference the tides are turned as the therapist now becomes idealized by the patient, elevated to a pedestal of absolute therapeutic power and perfection. In the twinship or alter ego transference, again as its alternate names imply, the patient assumes that his or her own personal convictions, thoughts, and feelings are identical to those held or experienced by the therapist.

Kohut determined that these narcissistic transferences represented defensive strategies by which patients compensated for specific deficits in their own self structure. Those who demanded perfect mirroring and idealization from the therapist, Kohut reasoned, must lack internal support for their own ambitions as well as the emotional capacity to soothe or affirm themselves. Patients who idealized the therapist's perfection were shoring up uncertainty in the realm of their own guiding ideals and convictions. Other patients who assumed the perfect similarity of the therapist, Kohut inferred, must lack the capacity to trust or to engage their own talents and skills.

These defensive patterns led Kohut (1977, p. 180; Kohut and Wolf, 1986, p. 177) to speculate on the bipolar, possibly tripolar, structure of the vital self. The first of these poles, which Kohut called the *grandiose self*, generates the self's basic strivings and ambitions; from the second pole, or *idealizing parent image*, emanate the self's guiding principles and idealized goals; and the dynamic, almost electrical tension-arc of energy between these two poles—and perhaps a third pole in its own right, known in Kohut's later writings as the *twinship self*—is composed of the unique talents and skills by which the self pursues its ambitions while striving to honor its ideals. The healthy self, for Kohut, is *pushed* or *driven* by its ambitions, *pulled* or *upheld* by its ideals, and *mediated* or *integrated* by its talents and skills.

If parents and the wider social environment respond with nurturing empathy to the legitimate needs of young children's grandiose, idealizing, and twinship selves—if, that is, children can bask in their parents' acceptance, are permitted to idealize their parents' competence, or are allowed to treasure the camaraderie of a special, often imaginary, friend—these three rudimentary selves eventually become transformed into children's growing pleasure in pursuing their own particular ambitions, striving toward their ideals, and utilizing their talents and skills, all of these abilities signifying what Kohut considered to be aspects of healthy narcissism. The vigorous self, from this perspective, *requires acceptance, feels a part of greatness*, and *cherishes camaraderie* (Dykstra, 1997, pp. 62; 131, n. 25).

If, however, the early childhood environment proves traumatically unempathic or grossly unresponsive to these archaic needs, as Kohut believed to have been the case in the early lives of his patients, then the more primitive forms of grandiosity and idealization fail to become adequately internalized and modulated. In these cases, the narcissistically vulnerable person continues to require ongoing support from a steady cadre of external selfobjects to shore up a fragile sense of self (Kohut, 1971, pp. 69ff., 98ff., 121).

Kohut saw his therapeutic role, then, as one of restorative empathy, that is, as one of providing for such patients precisely what they lacked from childhood selfobjects and now demanded of others. For the grandiose patient, Kohut-as-therapist sought to be, for quite some time, little more than an affirming mirror; for the idealizing patient, he allowed himself to accept the patient's idealization; for the twinship patient, he tolerated the patient's assumptions of their perfect similarity.

In assuming this unnatural relational stance under adverse therapeutic conditions, however, Kohut recognized that at some point he inevitably would fail to sustain perfect empathy. In these instances, the patient would become agitated and respond with hypersensitive rage or shame. Kohut discovered, however, that far from harming the patient, these failures of empathy, if relatively minor and if recognized and consequently "confessed" by the therapist and discussed with the patient, actually led to the growth of the patient's own self and capacity for self-soothing. At such moments of an acknowledged failure to understand the patient, Kohut believed that small "particles" of the therapist's healthy self were somehow transferred to the patient's enfeebled self (Kohut, 1984, p. 78). He called this phenomenon *transmuting internalization*, a technical term for the painstaking relational process by which patients become increasingly capable of regulating their shame and rage—*of holding themselves together*—in the face of minor injuries or affronts to the self.

The satisfying results of therapy with a person suffering from a narcissistic self disorder, according to Kohut (1984, p. 76), become evident in "an analysand's increased capacity to be reassured by a friend's wordlessly putting his arm around his shoulder, his newly obtained or rekindled ability to feel strengthened and uplifted when listening to music, his broadened sense of being in tune with the preoccupations of a group to which he belongs, his liberated ability to exhibit joyfully the products of his creativity in order to obtain the approval of a responsive selfobject audience." These transformations of narcissism do not necessarily mean that the patient will experience enhanced success in intimate relationships. In reiterating his convictions concerning the importance of healthy narcissism, however, Kohut pointed to countless creative persons in history who, although unsuccessful in intimacy, made vast contributions to the human artistic, scientific, and spiritual endowment (Kohut, 1978, pp. 617–18; and Kohut, 1987, pp. 3–30).

Kohut affirmed, then, not as selfish but as essential, three great constellations of the human self: the grandiose self and its *need to find acceptance reflected in the face of another*; the idealizing self and its *desire to become enveloped in the greatness and infallibility of another*; and the twinship self and its *joy in discovering someone experienced not as superior or subordinate but as equal companion and friend.* These three "selves" that together make for healthy narcissism continue to seek confirmation and transformation not just in early childhood but throughout the whole of one's life (Dykstra, 1997, pp. 61–62; 131, n. 25). This juncture, then, brings us full circle to consider areas of convergence between Kohut's self psychology and Bailey's metaphorical theology.

The Self as the Wedding of Waters

Self psychology resonates with Bailey's rendering of Jesus' parables of Luke 15 in at least two important regards, each in turn corresponding with what Kohut considered his two primary contributions to contemporary psychoanalytic theory and therapy. The first area of convergence involves what Kohut perceived as the influential, even essential, role of narcissism and positive self-regard throughout the whole of one's life. Kohut almost certainly would have affirmed the twin aspects of vital selfhood gleaned from Bailey's depictions of the protagonists of the parables—a shepherd, a woman, and a father who, on the one hand, clearly make significant personal sacrifices in order to restore lost others, but who also, on the other hand, shamelessly seek to celebrate their own achievements in ultimately having found the objects of their concern.

Kohut would find here theological confirmation for his conception of the self's two parallel lines of development (Kohut, 1971, p. 220; and Kohut, 1978, pp. 617–19). One of these entails an evolving maturity in the realm of object relations, that is, in the self's increasing ability to relate lovingly to others—evident in one's capacity, say, to search out the lost and to experience communion and self-transcendence. The other line of development, we have seen, involves the gradual emergence of healthy narcissism, that is, of the self's increasing ability to regulate self-esteem in the face of shame and other personal affronts and to take pleasure in its own ambitions, talents, and ideals. Healthy narcissism enables an individual to celebrate her or his own accomplishments, to experience individuation and immanence, and to accept one's finitude. As Bailey proposes an image of a God who searches out others not only for the sake of the lost but also for the sake of God's own honor, so too Kohut affirms the contribution of healthy narcissism to psychological well-being (Kohut, 1987, pp. 5ff.). He seeks to reclaim narcissism from its tarnished reputation both in clinical psychology and in the popular imagination and to demonstrate narcissism's separate line of development independent of the self's growing capacity to love and nurture others.

A second area of convergence with Bailey's interpretation of Luke 15 is evident in Kohut's therapeutic approach. In this, Kohut echoes something of Jesus' sensitivity to the magnitude of the helplessness of the lost and depleted self and to its relative passivity in coming again to be found. Although Kohut (1977) likely would have preferred the term "restoration" to that of "repentance," he would have appreciated Bailey's definition, or Jesus' redefinition, of the self's repentance, restoration, or salvation as its *acceptance of being found*. Kohut's clinical descriptions of persons experiencing severe self disorders reflect Bailey's similar emphasis on the costly quality of the love—or, for Kohut, the empathy—necessary to restore such a self to vital integrity.

Kohut viewed self psychology's principal *theoretical* contribution as that of its perceiving the positive influence of narcissism on the self; he believed self psychology's primary *clinical* contribution to be its "discovery" of the central function of empathy in healing the self. Kohut equated empathy—the natural and learned ability to feel and think one's way into the internal life of another—with therapy: "Empathy is the operation that defines the field of psychoanalysis" (Kohut, 1984, p. 174); it is the "oxygen of the psyche," the foundation for human hope (Kohut, 1985, p. 222). He nonetheless remained acutely aware in working with persons suffering from pathological narcissism that maintaining such empathy severely taxes the therapist; for Kohut, as for Jesus in the parables of Luke 15, *the self is a deeply relational gift and task* whose formation and maturation come at considerable cost to its primary proponent and counterplayer in creation and redemption—to the mother or therapist in self psychology; to the shepherd, woman, and father (or to Jesus or God) in Christian theology.

The two distinctive colors of the Brazilian Amazon's waters converge at a place of great beauty and mystery but also of potent if submersed conflict and instability. So too in Jesus' parables and in Kohut's psychology one finds the self as a place of discordant wonder where collide one's temporality and one's transcendence, one's desires and one's ideals, one's intensity and one's dispassion, one's narcissistic self-concern and one's loving concern for others. In both Bailey and Kohut we find not an independent, free-standing, or firmly established self created somehow *ex nihilo*, but rather a self more tenuously fashioned from the stuff of a differentiated dyad—from a relationship akin to one between mother and child, between therapist and patient, between shepherd and sheep, between father and son, between Creator and creation.[4] The self appears at that dramatic but permeable frontier where those who desire meet the one whom they desire, where those hopelessly lost accept their coming selflessly to be found, and where eventually, perhaps eschatologically, the waters unite as one, and (to mix a metaphor or two) all feast assured of their bringing undisguised delight to the Source of their delight.

---

4. Pastoral theologian James E. Dittes (1996) observes that this differentiation of role reflects the relationship between Jesus and God: "When the early church fathers labored for centuries to formulate their understanding of the nature of Godhood, it was Jesus' distinctive role as Son that they struggled most to preserve. They needed to be able to speak of 'God the Son' as readily as 'God the Father'. But how could Jesus be fully God, yet son to a father God? That was not easy to answer. . . . But they were clear about what was at stake: Jesus had an identity as Son that it was essential to affirm as both distinct and divine. Distinct: The Son (like all sons) was at risk of being merged into his father's identity, but that must not be allowed, they intuited, lest important and unique saving power be lost. And divine: Jesus was no less divine for being Son." (p. 127). Although a more thorough exploration is beyond the scope of this chapter, worth noting is that this emphasis on the self-constituting power of an empathic differentiated dyad raises the important question of the contribution both of the individual's biological nature and of the larger society (the "village crowds" of the parables of Luke 15) to the formation and restoration of the self. Both Bailey and Kohut appear ambivalent in their discussions concerning the social construction of the self (Dykstra, 1997, p. 55).

References

Allport, G. W. (1950). *The individual and his religion.* New York, NY: Macmillan.

American Psychiatric Association. (2013). *Diagnostic and statistical manual of mental disorders* (5th ed.). Washington, DC: American Psychiatric Association.

Arjona Mejía, R. J. (2017). *The minister as curator of desire: A model of pastoral accompaniment with young Mexican men* (Unpublished doctoral dissertation). Princeton Theological Seminary, Princeton, NJ.

Armstrong, K. (2000). *The battle for God: Fundamentalism in Judaism, Christianity, and Islam.* New York, NY: Knopf.

Bailey, K. E. (1992). *Finding the lost: Cultural keys to Luke 15.* Concordia scholarship today. St. Louis, MO: Concordia.

Bakan, D. (1966). *The duality of human existence: Isolation and communion in Western man.* Boston, MA: Beacon.

Barthes, R. (1982). *Image, music, text.* Flamingo 4067. London, UK: Fontana Paperbacks.

Bellah, R. N., Madsen, R., Sullivan, W. M., Swidler, A., & Tipton, S. M. (1985). *Habits of the heart: Individualism and commitment in American life.* Berkeley, CA: University of California Press.

Billig, M. (1999). *Freudian repression: Conversation creating the unconscious.* Cambridge, UK: Cambridge University Press.

Bilton, N. (2015, February 25). Strippers go undercover on Snapchat. *New York Times.* http://www.nytimes.com/2015/02/26/style/strippers-go-undercover-on-snapchat.html/.

Black, R. D. (2016, Nov. 27). Why I left white nationalism. *New York Times.* Retrieved from https://www.nytimes.com/2016/11/26/opinion/sunday/why-i-left-white-nationalism.html?_r=0/.

Brainerd Dispatch. (2001). Dr. Harold August Christiansen. Retrieved from http://www.brainerddispatch.com/content/dr-harold-august-christiansen/.

Bronfen, E. (1992). *Over her dead body: Death, femininity, and the aesthetic.* New York, NY: Routledge.

Brooks, M. (2006a). *World War Z: An oral history of the zombie war.* New York, NY: Crown.

Brooks, M. (2006b, Oct. 6). Zombie wars. *Washington Post.* Retrieved from http://www.washingtontonpost.com/wp-dyn/content/discussion/2003/10/26/DI2005033114558.html/.

Brown, N. O. (1985). *Life against death: The psychoanalytical meaning of history.* Middletown, CT: Wesleyan University Press.

References

Buechner, F. (1973). *Wishful thinking: A theological ABC*. New York, NY: Harper & Row.

———. (1991). *Telling secrets: A memoir*. San Francisco, CA: HarperSanFrancisco.

Butler, L. H., Jr. (2010). *Listen, my son: Wisdom for African American fathers*. Nashville, TN: Abingdon.

Cain, A. C., & Fast, I. (1972). Children's disturbed reaction to parent suicide. In A. C. Cain (Ed.), *Survivors of suicide*. Springfield, IL: Thomas.

Caird, G. B. (1963). *The Gospel of St. Luke*. Pelican Gospel Commentaries. New York, NY: Seabury.

Campbell, A. V. (1981). *Rediscovering pastoral care*. Philadelphia, PA: Westminster.

Capps, D. (1983). *Life cycle theory and pastoral care*. Theology and pastoral care series. Philadelphia, PA: Fortress.

———. (1993). *The depleted self: Sin in a narcissistic age*. Minneapolis, MN: Fortress.

———. (1995). *The child's song: The religious abuse of children*. Louisville, KY: Westminster John Knox.

———. (1997). *Men, religion, and melancholia: James, Otto, Jung, and Erikson*. New Haven, CT: Yale University Press.

———. (1998). *Living stories: Pastoral counseling in congregational context*. Minneapolis, MN: Fortress.

———. (2001). Male melancholia: Guilt, separation, and repressed rage. In D. Jonte-Pace & W. B. Parsons (Eds.), *Religion and psychology: Mapping the terrain* (pp. 147–59). London, UK: Routledge.

———. (2008). *Jesus the village psychiatrist*. Louisville, KY: Westminster John Knox.

———. (2013). *At home in the world: A study in psychoanalysis, religion, and art*. Eugene, OR: Cascade Books.

———. (2014a). *Still growing: The creative self in older adulthood*. Eugene, OR: Cascade Books.

———. (2014b). Method, models, and scholarly types: Reflections on thesis and dissertation writing in pastoral theology. *Pastoral Psychology, 63*, 551–60. https://doi.org/10.1007/s11089-014-0594-4

———. (2015). *The religious life: The insights of William James*. Eugene, OR: Cascade Books.

Carlin, N. (2014). *Religious mourning: Reversals and restorations in psychological portraits of religious leaders*. Eugene, OR: Wipf & Stock.

Carlin, N., & Capps, D. (2015). *The gift of sublimation: A psychoanalytic study of multiple masculinities*. Eugene, OR: Cascade Books.

Chapman, J. J. (1996). William James. In L. Simon (Ed.), *William James remembered* (pp. 50–57). Lincoln, NE: University of Nebraska Press.

Coltart, N. (1992). *Slouching towards Bethlehem*. New York, NY: Guilford.

Cooper. T. D., & Randall, R. L. (2011). *Grace for the injured self: The healing approach of Heinz Kohut*. Eugene, OR: Pickwick Publications.

Cotkin, G. (1994). *William James: Public philosopher*. Urbana, IL: University of Illinois Press.

Craddock, F. B. (1990). *Luke*. Interpretation: A Bible commentary for teaching and preaching. Louisville, KY: Westminster John Knox.

Culpepper, R. A. (1995). *Luke/John*. The new interpreter's Bible 9. Nashville, TN: Abingdon.

Dittes, J. E. (1996). *Driven by hope: Men and meaning.* Louisville, KY: Westminster John Knox.

Doehring, C. (2015). *The practice of pastoral care: A postmodern approach* (revised and expanded). Louisville, KY: Westminster John Knox.

Dornisch, L. C. (2002). *A woman reads the Gospel of Luke.* Collegeville, MN: Liturgical.

Du Bois, W. E. B. (1940). *Dusk of dawn: An essay toward an autobiography of a race concept.* New York, NY: Harcourt, Brace.

Dunstan, S. (1991). *Christus paradox.* Chicago, IL: GIA.

Dykstra, R. C. (1997). *Counseling troubled youth.* Louisville, KY: Westminster John Knox.

———. (2001). *Discovering a sermon: Personal pastoral preaching.* St. Louis, MO: Chalice.

———. (2005). *Images of pastoral care: Classic readings.* St. Louis, MO: Chalice.

———. (2009). Subversive friendship. *Pastoral Psychology, 58,* 579–601. https://doi.org/10.1007/s11089-009-0253-3.

Dykstra, R. C., Cole, A. H., Jr., & Capps, D. (2007). *Losers, loners, and rebels: The spiritual struggles of boys.* Louisville, KY: Westminster John Knox.

Dykstra, R. C., Cole A. H., Jr., & Capps, D. (2012). *The faith and friendships of teenage boys.* Louisville, KY: Westminster John Knox.

Edmundson, M. (2007). *The death of Sigmund Freud: The legacy of his last days.* New York, NY: Bloomsbury.

———. (2013). *Why teach? In defense of a real education.* New York, NY: Bloomsbury.

Ellison, G. C., II. (2013). *Cut dead but still alive: Caring for African American young men.* Nashville, TN: Abingdon.

Emerson, R. W. (1946/1981). *The portable Emerson* (Rev. ed.). Carl Bode (Ed.). New York, NY: Penguin.

Erikson, E. H. (1968). *Identity, youth, and crisis.* New York, NY: Norton.

———. (1974). *Dimensions of a new identity.* The 1973 Jefferson lectures in the humanities. New York, NY: Norton.

———. (1981). The Galilean sayings and the sense of 'I'. *Yale Review, 70,* 321–62.

Eton, L. (2006, Oct. 2). Zombies spreading like a virus: PW talks with Max Brooks. *Publisher's Weekly.* http://www.publishersweekly.com/article/CA6376416.html/.

Evans, E. G. (1996). William James and his wife. In L. Simon (Ed.), *William James remembered* (pp. 58–81). Lincoln, NE: University of Nebraska Press.

Evodokimov, P. (1985). *The sacrament of love.* Crestwood, NY: St. Vladimir's Seminary Press.

Fadiman, A. (1997). *The spirit catches you and you fall down: A Hmong child, her American doctors, and the collision of two cultures.* New York, NY: Farrar, Straus & Giroux.

Fitzmyer, J. A. (1986). *The Gospel according to Luke* (Vol. 2). Anchor Bible 28A. Garden City, NY: Doubleday.

Forster, M. (Director). (2013). *World War Z* [Motion picture]. United States: Paramount.

Freud, S. (1909/1990). Analysis of a phobia in a five-year-old boy. In *Case studies I.* Penguin Freud library 8. Harmondsworth, UK: Penguin.

———. (1915/2005). Timely reflections on war and death. In *On murder, mourning and melancholia.* A. Phillips (Ed.). Modern classics. The new Penguin Freud. London, UK: Penguin.

———. (1917/1957). Mourning and melancholia. In J. Strachey (Ed.), *The standard edition of the complete psychological works of Sigmund Freud* (Vol. 14, pp. 239–57). London, UK: Hogarth.

REFERENCES

——. (1923a/1960). The ego and the id. In J. Strachey (Ed.), J. Riviere (Trans.). *The standard edition of the complete works of Sigmund Freud* (Vol. 19, pp. 13–68). New York, NY: Norton.

——. (1923b/1984). The ego and the id. In *On metapsychology*. The Penguin Freud library 11. Harmondsworth, UK: Penguin.

——. (1924/1986). An autobiographical study. In *Historical and Expository Works on Psychoanalysis*. Penguin Freud library 15. Harmondsworth, UK: Penguin.

——. (1929/1989). *Civilization and its discontents*. In *The standard edition of the complete works of Sigmund Freud*. J. Strachey (Ed. & Trans.). New York, NY: Norton.

——. (1933a/1965). *New introductory lectures on psychoanalysis*. J. Strachey (Ed. & Trans.). New York, NY: Norton.

——. (1933b/1987). *New introductory lectures on psychoanalysis*. Penguin Freud library 2. Hammondsworth, UK: Penguin.

Freud, S., & Jung, C. G. (1979). *The Freud/Jung letters: The correspondence between Sigmund Freud and C. G. Jung* (Abridged ed.). W. McGuire (Ed.). Princeton/Bollingen series. Bollingen series 94. Princeton, NJ: Princeton University Press.

Freudenthal, T. (Director). (2013). *Percy Jackson: Sea of monsters* [Motion picture]. United States: 20th Century Fox.

Furman, B., & Ahola, T. (1992). *Solution talk: Hosting therapeutic conversations*. New York, NY: Norton.

Gilbert, D. (2006). *Stumbling on happiness*. New York, NY: Vintage.

González, J. L. (2010). *Luke*. Belief: A Theological Commentary on the Bible. Louisville, KY: Westminster John Knox.

Green, J. (2010, Oct. 25). The intelligent homosexual's guide to himself. *New York Magazine*. http://nymag.com/arts/theater/profiles/68994/.

Green, J. B. (1997). *The Gospel of Luke*. The new international commentary on the New Testament. Grand Rapids, MI: Eerdmans.

Greene, G. (1940/1980). *The power and the glory*. New York, NY: Penguin.

Greenfield, J. (2012). Scholastic's hit-maker David Levithan on Hunger Games, digital reading and transmedia. Retrieved from http://www.digitalbookworld.com/2012/scholastics-hit-maker-david-levithan-on-hunger-games-digital-reading-and-transmedia/.

Gutheil, T. G., & Gabbard, G. O. (1993). The concept of boundaries in clinical practice: Theoretical and risk-management dimensions. *American Journal of Psychiatry, 150*, 188–96.

Haber, S. (2003). A woman's touch: Feminist encounters with the hemorrhaging woman in Mark 5:24–34. *Journal for the Study of the New Testament, 26*, 171–92.

Hale, N. G., Jr. (1971). *James Jackson Putnam and Psychoanalysis: Letters between Putnam and Sigmund Freud, Ernest Jones, William James, Sandor Ferenczi, and Morton Prince, 1877–1917*. Cambridge, MA: Harvard University Press.

Hand, D. (Director). (1937). *Snow White and the seven dwarfs* [Motion picture]. United States: Walt Disney Productions.

Hauerwas, S. (2006). *Matthew*. Brazos theological commentary on the Bible. Grand Rapids, MI: Brazos.

Helsel, P. B. (2015). *Pastoral power beyond psychology's marginalization: Resisting the discourses of the psy-complex*. New York, NY: Palgrave Macmillan.

Hiltner, S. (1958). *Preface to pastoral theology*. Nashville, TN: Abingdon.

Hinds, J.-P. (2010). Traces on the blackboard: The vestiges of racism on the African American psyche. *Pastoral Psychology, 59,* 783–98.

Hinds, J.-P. (2014). Shame and its sons: Black men, fatherhood, and filicide. *Pastoral Psychology, 63,* 641–58.

Hollingsworth, A. (2005). *The simple faith of Mister Rogers: Spiritual insights from the world's most beloved neighbor.* Nashville, TN: Integrity.

Horovitz, B. (2007, April 30). Marketers zooming in on your daily routines. *USA Today.* http://usatoday30.usatoday.com/printedition/news/20070430/1a_cover30.art.htm/.

Howe, M. A. D. (1937). *John Jay Chapman and his letters.* Boston, MA: Houghton Mifflin.

Hughes, T. (1995). Ted Hughes, the art of poetry No. 71. Interviewed by Drue Heinz. *The Paris Review, 134.* http://www.theparisreview.org/interviews/1669/the-art-of-poetry-no-71-ted-hughes/.

Jackson, P. (Director). (2012). *The hobbit: An unexpected journey* [Motion Picture]. United States: Warner Bros. Pictures.

James, H. (2016). *Henry James: Autobiographies.* P. Horne (Ed.). Library of America. New York, NY: Library of America.

James, H., III. (1996). A firm, light step. In L. Simon (Ed.), *William James remembered* (pp. 116–21). Lincoln, NE: University of Nebraska Press.

James, W. (1884). On some omissions of introspective psychology. *Mind, 9,* 1–26.

———. (1890/1983b). *The principles of psychology.* The Works of William James. Cambridge, MA: Harvard University Press.

———. (1892/1992). *Psychology: Briefer course.* In G. E. Myers (Ed.), *William James: Writings 1878–1899* (pp. 1–443). New York, NY: Library of America.

———. (1896/1956). *The will to believe, and other essays in popular philosophy.* New York, NY: Dover.

———. (1899/1958). On a certain blindness in human beings. In W. James, *Talks to teachers on psychology: And to students on some of life's ideals* (pp. 149–69). Norton library. New York, NY: Norton.

———. (1902/1982b). *The varieties of religious experience: A study in human nature.* The Penguin American library. New York, NY: Penguin.

———. (1907/2003). *Pragmatism: A new name for some old ways of thinking.* Barnes & Noble library of essential reading. New York, NY: Barnes & Noble.

———. (1982a). *Essays in religion and morality.* In F. H. Burkhardt, F. Bowers, and I. K. Skrupskelis (Eds.). The works of William James (Vol. 9). Cambridge, MA: Harvard University Press.

———. (1983a). *Essays in psychology.* In F. H. Burkhardt, F. Bowers, and I. K. Skrupskelis (Eds.), *The works of William James* (Vol. 11). Cambridge, MA: Harvard University Press.

Jeffrey, D. L. (2012). *Luke.* Brazos theological commentary on the Bible. Grand Rapids, MI: Brazos.

Jeremias, J. (1969). *Jerusalem in the time of Jesus.* Philadelphia, PA: Fortress.

Johnson, D. (1996, April 22). Students still sweat, they just don't shower. *New York Times.* http://www.nytimes.com/1996/04/22/us/students-still-sweat-they-just-don-t-shower.html/.

Johnson, L. T. (1991). *The Gospel of Luke.* Sacra Pagina Series 3. Collegeville, MN: Liturgical.

Jolly, R. (2009). Writing desire responsibly. In E. Boehmer, R. Eaglestone, & K. Iddiols (Eds.), *J. M. Coetzee in context and theory* (pp. 93–111). Continuum literary studies series. London, UK: Bloomsbury.

Jordan, M. D. (2003). *Telling truths in church: Scandal, flesh, and Christian speech.* Boston, MA: Beacon.

Juergensmeyer, M. (2003). *Terror in the mind of God: The global rise of religious violence* (3rd ed. revised and updated). Comparative studies in religion and society 13. Berkeley, CA: University of California Press.

Junod, T. (1998, November). Can you say . . . hero? *Esquire, 130*(5), 1432–39. Academic Search Premier database. http://www.esquire.com/entertainment/tv/interviews/a27134/can-you-say-hero-esq1198/.

Just, A. A., Jr. (Ed.). (2003). *Luke.* Ancient Christian commentary on Scripture, New Testament 3. Downers Grove, IL: InterVarsity.

Karen, R. (2001). *The forgiving self: The road from resentment to connection.* New York, NY: Doubleday.

Kearney, R. (2014, August 31). Losing our touch. *The Opinionator* (blog). *New York Times,* p. 4SR. Retrieved from https://opinionator.blogs.nytimes.com/2014/08/30/losing-our-touch/.

Kim, S. S. (2009). Individualism and collectivism: Implications for women. *Pastoral Psychology, 58,* 563–78. https://doi.org/10.1007/s11089-009-0236-4/.

Kinukawa, H. (1994). The story of the hemorrhaging woman (Mark 5:25–34) read from a Japanese feminist context. *Biblical Interpretation, 2,* 283–93.

Kleinman, A. (1980). *Patients and healers in the context of culture: An exploration of the borderland between anthropology, medicine, and psychiatry.* Comparative studies of health systems and medical care 3. Berkeley, CA: University of California Press.

Kohut, H. (1971). *The analysis of the self: A systematic approach to the psychoanalytic treatment of narcissistic personality disorders.* The psychoanalytic study of the child 4. New York, NY: International Universities Press.

———. (1977). *The restoration of the self.* New York, NY: International Universities Press.

———. (1978). *The search for the self: Selected writings of Heinz Kohut, 1950–1978* (Vol. 2). P. H. Ornstein (Ed.) Madison, CT: International Universities Press.

———. (1984). *How does analysis cure?* A. Goldberg (Ed.). Chicago, IL: University of Chicago Press.

———. (1985). *Self psychology and the humanities: Reflections on a new psychoanalytic approach.* C. B. Strozier (Ed.). New York, NY: Norton.

———. (1987). *The Kohut seminars on self psychology and psychotherapy with adolescents and young adults.* M. Elson (Ed.). New York, NY: Norton.

Kohut, H., & Wolf, E. S. (1986). The disorders of the self and their treatment: An outline. In A. P. Morrison (Ed.), *Essential papers on narcissism.* Essential papers in psychoanalysis. New York, NY: New York University Press.

Konnikova, M. (2014, June 2). What's lost as handwriting fades. *New York Times.* Retrieved from http://www.nytimes.com/2014/06/03/science/whats-lost-as-handwriting-fades.html?_r=0/.

Kristeva, J. (1992). *Black sun: Depression and melancholia.* L. S. Roudiez (Trans.). European perspectives. New York, NY: Columbia University Press.

Kujawa-Holbrook, S. A., & Montagno, K. B. (Eds.). (2009). *Injustice and the care of souls: Taking oppression seriously in pastoral care.* Minneapolis, MN: Fortress.

LaMothe, R. (2013). *Missing us: Re-visioning psychoanalysis from the perspective of community*. Lanham, MD: Aronson.

Lartey, E. Y. (2006). *Pastoral theology in an intercultural world*. Cleveland, OH: Pilgrim.

Lee, A. (Director). (2005). *Brokeback mountain* [Motion Picture]. United States: Universal.

Leslie, K. J. (2003). *When violence is no stranger: Pastoral counseling with survivors of acquaintance rape*. Minneapolis, MN: Fortress.

Lewis, R. W. B. (1991). *The Jameses: A family narrative*. London: Deutsch.

Lifton, R. J. (1993). *The protean self: Human resilience in an age of fragmentation*. New York, NY: Basic Books.

Madigan, T. (2006). *I'm proud of you: My friendship with Fred Rogers*. New York, NY: Gotham.

Malbon, E. S. (1983). Fallible followers: Women and men in the Gospel of Mark. *Semeia, 28*, 29–48.

Marshall, J. L. (1997). *Counseling lesbian partners*. Counseling and pastoral theology. Louisville, KY: Westminster John Knox.

Martin, D. B. (2006). *Sex and the single savior: Gender and sexuality in biblical interpretation*. Louisville, KY: Westminster John Knox.

Martinez, D. (2012). *The boy kings of Texas: A memoir*. Guilford, CT: Lyons.

McClure, B. J. (2010). *Moving beyond individualism in pastoral care and counseling: Reflections on theory, theology, and practice*. Eugene, OR: Cascade Books.

McDargh, J. (1995). Desire, domination, and the life and death of the soul. In R. K. Fenn & D. Capps (Eds.), *On losing the soul: Essays in the social psychology of religion* (pp. 213–30). Albany, NY: State University of New York Press.

McWhirter, J. (2013). *Rejected prophets: Jesus and his witnesses in Luke–Acts*. Minneapolis, MN: Fortress.

Mencken, H. L. (1949/1982). *A Mencken chrestomathy*. New York, NY: Vintage.

Meyer, R. (2014, November 2). The most popular passages in books, according to Kindle data. *Atlantic Monthly*. https://www.theatlantic.com/technology/archive/2014/11/the-passages-that-readers-love/381373/.

Micale, M. S. (1995). *Approaching hysteria: Disease and its implications*. Princeton, NJ: Princeton University Press.

Miller, A. (1981/2008). *The drama of the gifted child: The search for the true self*. R. Ward (Trans.). New York, NY: Basic Books.

———. (1991). *Breaking down the wall of silence: The liberating experience of facing painful truths*. S. Worrall (Trans.). New York, NY: Dutton.

———. (2001). *The truth will set you free: Overcoming emotional blindness and finding your true adult self*. New York, NY: Basic Books.

Miller, J. W. (1997). *Jesus at thirty: A psychological and historical portrait*. Minneapolis, MN: Fortress.

Miller-McLemore, B. J. (1996). The living human web: Pastoral theology at the turn of the century. In J. S. Moessner (Ed.), *Through the eyes of women: Insights for pastoral care* (pp. 9–26). Minneapolis, MN: Fortress.

———. (2003). *Let the children come: Reimagining childhood from a Christian perspective*. Families and faith series. San Francisco, CA: Jossey-Bass.

Miller-McLemore, B. J., & Gill-Austern, B. L. (Eds.). (1999). *Feminist and womanist pastoral theology*. Nashville, TN: Abingdon.

Moore, S. (2007). *The contagion of Jesus: Doing theology as if it mattered*. Maryknoll, NY: Orbis.

Murdoch, I. (2001). *The sovereignty of good*. Routledge classics. London: Routledge.

Myers, G. E. (1986). *William James: His life and thought*. New Haven, CT: Yale University Press.

———. (1997). Pragmatism and introspective psychology. In R. A. Putnam (Ed.), *The Cambridge companion to William James* (pp. 11–24). Cambridge, UK: Cambridge University Press.

Nelson, C. E. (1989). *How faith matures*. Louisville, KY: Westminster John Knox.

Nouwen, H. J. M. (1990). *In the name of Jesus: Reflections on Christian leadership*. New York, NY: Crossroad.

Ogas, O. (2011, June 5). Why it's perfectly natural for men to want to show their manhood, even if it's a bad idea: Congressman Weiner behaves like any other male primate. *Psychology Today*. https://www.psychologytoday.com/blog/billion-wicked-thoughts/201106/why-its-perfectly-natural-men-want-show-their-manhood-even-if/.

Ogas, O., & Gaddam, S. (2012). *A billion wicked thoughts: What the Internet tells us about sexual relationships*. New York, NY: Plume.

O'Hanlon, B. (2009, March 26). Working with difficult clients. A lecture delivered at the Psychotherapy Networker Conference. Washington DC.

Perry, R. B. (1948/1996). *The thought and character of William James*. Vanderbilt library of American philosophy. Nashville, TN: Vanderbilt University Press.

Phillips, A. (1994). *On flirtation: Psychoanalytic essays on the uncommitted life*. Cambridge, MA: Harvard University Press.

———. (1995). *Terrors and experts*. Cambridge, MA: Harvard University Press.

———. (1998). *The beast in the nursery: On curiosity and other appetites*. New York, NY: Pantheon.

———. (2002). *Equals*. New York, NY: Basic Books.

———. (2005). *Going sane: Maps of happiness*. New York, NY: Fourth Estate/Harper Collins.

———. (2010). *On balance*. New York, NY: Farrar, Straus, and Giroux.

———. (2016). *Unforbidden pleasures*. New York, NY: Farrar, Straus and Giroux.

Pipher, M. (2015, March/April). Psychotherapy in the age of overwhelm. *Psychotherapy Networker*, 22–23.

Plummer, A. (1956). *A critical and exegetical commentary on the Gospel according to St. Luke*. International critical commentary series. Edinburgh, UK: T. & T. Clark.

Prochnik, G. (2006). *Putnam Camp: Sigmund Freud, James Jackson Putnam, and the purpose of American psychology*. New York, NY: Other Press.

Proulx, A. (2003). Brokeback mountain. In A. Proulx, *Close range: Wyoming stories* (pp. 253–85). New York, NY: Scribner.

Putnam, J. J. (1996). William James. In L. Simon (Ed.), *William James remembered* (pp. 7–26). Lincoln, NE: University of Nebraska Press.

Putnam, R. A. (Ed.). (1997). *The Cambridge companion to William James*. Cambridge, UK: Cambridge University Press.

Rabin, R. C. (2013, Aug. 12). A glut of antidepressants. *New York Times*. Retrieved from http://well.blogs.nytimes.com/2013/08/12/a-glut-of-antidepressants/?_php=true&_type=blogs&_r=0/.

Rambo, S. (2009). Trauma and faith: Reading the narrative of the hemorrhaging woman. *International Journal of Practical Theology*, 13, 233–57.

REFERENCES

Ramsay, N. J. (Ed.). (2004). *Pastoral care and counseling: Redefining the paradigms.* Nashville, TN: Abingdon.

Rangell, L. (1982). The self in psychoanalytic theory. *Journal of the American Psychoanalytic Association, 30,* 863–91.

Rehm, D. (2009, September 12). Thirty years of the unexpected. *Weekend Edition.* National Public Radio. http://www.npr.org/templates/story/story.php?storyId=112758776.

Reid, B. E. (1996). *Choosing the better part? Women in the Gospel of Luke.* Collegeville, MN: Liturgical.

———. (2000). *Parables for Preachers: Year C.* Collegeville, MN: Liturgical.

Remnick, D. (2012, July 30). We are alive: Bruce Springsteen at sixty-two. *New Yorker,* 38–57. http://www.newyorker.com/magazine/2012/07/30/we-are-alive/.

Richardson, R. D. (2006). *William James: In the maelstrom of American modernism.* Boston, MA: Houghton Mifflin.

Richtel, M. (2013, September 21). Intimacy on the Web, with a crowd. *New York Times.* Retrieved from http://www.nytimes.com/2013/09/22/technology/intimacy-on-the-web-with-a-crowd.html/.

Rieff, P. (1966/2006). *The triumph of the therapeutic: Uses of faith after Freud.* Wilmington, DE: Intercollegiate Studies Institute.

Ringe, S. H. (1995). *Luke.* Westminster Bible companion. Louisville, KY: Westminster John Knox.

Rogers, C. R. (1961). *On becoming a person: A therapist's view of psychotherapy.* Boston, MA: Houghton Mifflin.

Rogers, F. (1997). Fred Rogers acceptance speech, 1997. http://lybio.net/tag/fred-rogers-acceptance-speech-1997-transcription/.

———. (2014). Tragic events. http://www.fci.org/new-site/par-tragic-events.html/.

Roughgarden, J. (2004). *Evolution's rainbow: Diversity, gender, and sexuality in nature and people.* Berkeley, CA: University of California Press.

Rowling, J. K. (2000). *Harry Potter and the goblet of fire.* New York, NY: Scholastic.

———. (2007). *Harry Potter and the deathly hallows.* New York: Arthur A. Levine Books.

Royce, J. (1996). A word of greeting to William James. In L. Simon (Ed.), *William James remembered* (pp. 36–42). Lincoln, NE: University of Nebraska Press.

Ruvolo, J. (2011, September 7). How much of the Internet is actually for porn. *Forbes.* Retrieved from http://www.forbes.com/sites/julieruvolo/2011/09/07/how-much-of-the-internet-is-actually-for-porn/.

Saslow, E. (2016, Oct. 15). The white flight of Derek Black. *Washington Post.* Retrieved from https://www.washingtonpost.com/national/the-white-flight-of-derek-black/2016/10/15/ed5f906a-8f3b-11e6-a6a3-d50061aa9fae_story.html?utm_term=.d308895c5cad/.

Schüssler Fiorenza, E. (1994). *In memory of her: A feminist theological reconstruction of Christian origins* (10th anniversary ed.). New York, NY: Crossroad.

Scott, B. B. (1989). *Hear then the parable: A commentary on the parables of Jesus.* Minneapolis, MN: Fortress.

Searle, J. (1992). *The rediscovery of the mind.* Representation and mind. Cambridge, MA: MIT Press.

Shakespeare, W. (1997/2007). *King Lear.* R. A. Foakes (Ed.), The Arden Shakespeare. London, UK: Thomson Learning.

Shin, H.-U. (2012). *Vulnerability and courage: A pastoral theology of poverty and the alienated self.* Practical theology 3. New York, NY: Lang.

REFERENCES

Simon, L. (Ed.). (1996). *William James remembered.* Lincoln, NE: University of Nebraska Press.

Sinclair, S. (2015, February 8). Child, bride, mother. *New York Times.* Retrieved from http://www.nytimes.com/interactive/2015/02/08/opinion/sunday/exposures-child-bride-mother-stephanie-sinclair.html/.

Smith, D. (2012). *Monkey mind: A memoir of anxiety.* New York, NY: Simon & Schuster.

Smith-Rosenberg, C. (1981). The hysterical woman: Sex roles and role conflict in nineteenth-century America. In R. J. Brugger (Ed.), *Our selves/our past: Psychological approaches to American history* (pp. 205–27). Baltimore, MD: Johns Hopkins University Press.

Snodgrass, K. (2008). *Stories with intent: A comprehensive guide to the parables of Jesus.* Grand Rapids, MI: Eerdmans.

Spiegel, A. (2013, April 1). Mining books to map emotions through a century. *All Things Considered.* National Public Radio. http://www.npr.org/sections/health-shots/2013/04/01/175584297/mining-books-to-map-emotions-through-a-century.

Steinberg, L. (1996). *The sexuality of Christ in Renaissance art and in modern oblivion* (2nd ed.). Chicago, IL: University of Chicago Press.

Stevenson, R. L. (1892). *Across the plains: Leaves from the notebook of an emigrant between New York and San Francisco.* New York, NY: Charles Scribner's Sons.

Stevenson-Moessner, J. (1991). A new pastoral paradigm and practice. In M. Glaz & J. Stevenson-Moessner (Eds.), *Women in travail and transition: A new pastoral care* (pp. 198–211). Minneapolis, MN: Fortress.

Stevenson-Moessner, J., & Snorton, T. (Eds.). (2010). *Women out of order: Risking change and creating care in a multicultural world.* Minneapolis, MN: Fortress.

Stone, M. H. (1986). *Essential papers on borderline disorders.* Essential papers in psychoanalysis. New York, NY: New York University Press.

Strochlic, N. (2014, September 18). The sad plight of child grooms. *The Daily Beast.* Retrieved from http://www.thedailybeast.com/articles/2014/09/18/the-sad-hidden-plight-of-child-grooms.html#/.

Strozier, C. B., Terman, D. M., & Jones, J. W., with Boyd, K. A. (Eds.). (2010). *The fundamentalist mindset: Psychological perspectives on religion, violence, and history.* New York, NY: Oxford University Press.

Sweis, R. F. (2014, September 13). In Jordan, ever younger Syrian brides. *New York Times.* https://www.nytimes.com/2014/09/14/world/middleeast/in-jordan-ever-younger-syrian-brides.html/.

Tannehill, R. C. (1996). *Luke.* Abingdon New Testament commentaries. Nashville, TN: Abingdon.

Taylor, W. C. (2006, August 13). Get out of that rut and into the shower. *New York Times.* http://www.nytimes.com/2006/08/13/business/yourmoney/13mgmt.html?pagewanted=all&_r=0/.

Tillich, P. (1952). *The courage to be.* Terry Lectures. New Haven, CT: Yale University Press.

Tillman, L. (2012, November 9). Returning to the scene of a memoir. *New York Times.* http://www.nytimes.com/2012/11/10/books/domingo-martinez-takes-a-trip-back-to-south-texas.html/.

Townsend, K. (1996). *Manhood at Harvard: William James and others.* New York, NY: Norton.

Tripp, C. A. (2005). *The intimate world of Abraham Lincoln.* L. Gannett (Ed.). New York, NY: Free Press.

References

Vonnegut, M. (2002). *The Eden express: A memoir of insanity*. New York, NY: Seven Stories.

———. (2010). *Just like someone without mental illness only more so: A memoir*. New York, NY: Delacorte.

Ward, M. (2013, June 30). Web porn: just how much is there? *BBC News*. Retrieved from http://www.bbc.com/news/technology-23030090/.

Weingarten, G. (2007, April 8). Pearls before breakfast. *Washington Post*, 1A. https://www.washingtonpost.com/lifestyle/magazine/pearls-before-breakfast-can-one-of-the-nations-great-musicians-cut-through-the-fog-of-a-dc-rush-hour-lets-find-out/2014/09/23/8a6d46da-4331-11e4-b47c-f5889e061e5f_story.html?utm_term=.561c7e2e3f57/.

Whyte, D. (2009, March 29). Unpublished keynote address to the Psychotherapy Networker Symposium, Washington DC

Willimon, William H. (2013, February 20). Making ministry difficult: The goal of seminary. *Christian Century*, 11–12.

Wise, C. A. (1966). *The meaning of pastoral care*. New York, NY: Harper & Row.

Woodring, P. (1958). Introduction. In W. James (1899/1958), *Talks to teachers on psychology: And to students on some of life's ideals* (pp. 6–17). New York, NY: Norton.

Young, G. (2013, Aug. 25). The heroism of Antoinette Tuff reveals what's missing from politics. *The Guardian*. https://www.theguardian.com/commentisfree/2013/aug/25/antoinette-tuff-heroism-missing-from-politics/.

Young, R. M. (2002). Fundamentalism and terrorism. In J. S. Piven, P. Ziolo, & H. W. Lawton (Eds.), *Terror and apocalypse: Psychological undercurrents of history* (pp. 205–43). San Jose, CA: Writer's Showcase.

Index

Index

INDEX

Phillips, Adam
  on attending to one's inner
    fundamentalists, 31–32
  on avoiding important
    conversations, 64–65,
    100–101
  on ego as experiment in
    imagining, 34
  on humiliating children, 54
  on id and superego, 32, 83, 95
  on nature of sanity, 15, 114
  on paradox in psychotherapy,
    36–37
  on repression, 58
  on responding to extremism, 25,
    29–30, 37
  on self-listening in psychotherapy
    and art, 65
  on self-reproach as self-murder,
    82–83
  on shame as total conviction,
    75, 81
  on superego as internal critic,
    83, 95
  on symptoms as self-cure, 104
Pipher, Mary, 1, 13
Plato, 106
pluralism, 10, 17, 88, 95–96
poetry, 48–49, 53–54, 64, 71, 126
pornography, 103n1
postmodernism, 85
pragmatism, 84–85
prayer, 22–23, 115, 122–24
Princeton Theological Seminary, 12,
    14–16, 18–19, 26
Prochnik, George, 92
Proulx, Annie, 20
psychoanalysis, 41, 57–59, 61, 110,
    136–38, 142
psychological needs and concerns, 7,
    33, 51
psychology, 10
psychology of religion, 28–29
psychosis, 4, 44, 104–5
psychosomatic illness, 80, 104, 109,
    113; *see* somatic symptom
    disorders

psychotherapy, 5–6, 36, 41, 54–56,
    64, 114
Puritanism, 6
Putnam, Charles, 92
Putnam, James Jackson, 92, 93n2

racial concerns, 9
Rambo, Shelly, 106
religious discourse, 65
Remnick, David, 8
Renaissance painters, 119
repression, 32, 49, 54, 57–60, 62–64,
    66, 70–71
Richardson, Robert D., 78–79
Rogers, Carl R., 23–24, 41
Rogers, Fred, 12–13, 21–23, 42–43,
    116–18, 122–24
Rowling, J. K., 51
Royce, Josiah, 92

salvation, 11, 127, 134, 142
sanity, nature of, 15
scars, 117, 119, 121, 123
self
  acceptance of, 41, 73, 89, 96
  as boundary experience, 125–28
  bipolar/tripolar constitution of,
    32, 139, 141
  composite, 34–37
  depletion of, 132, 137
  ecumenical, 37–37, 40
  embracing shameful, 70
  empathy for, 142; *see* empathy
  esteem of, 136–37, 141
  fragmentation of, 138–40
  listening to one's own, 65
  loathing of, 3, 8, 13, 21, 81–82,
    93, 93n2, 95, 137
  metaphoric constitution of, 130
  murder of, 80–81
  need for stronger sense of, 85
  realization of, 52
  relational constitution of, 40–42,
    136, 138–9, 141–43, 143n4
  renunciation of, 73
  soothing of, 140–41
  transcendence of, 141

Scripture Index